# Getting Your Goat

**goat** [gəʊt]. Common Teutonic: Old English *gát*, feminine, = Middle Dutch *geit, geet(e)*, Dutch *geit* (obsolete *geite, geyte*), Old High German *geiz, keiz* (Middle High German *geiz*, modern German *geiß*, Old Norse *geit* (Swedish *get*, Danish *ged*), Gothic ɾʌɪᴛs *gait-s*: Old Teutonic \**gait-* cognate with Latin *hœdus* kid:—Indo-European \**ghaid-*. In Old English the vowel of the nominative singular remained in the genitive *gáte*, the genitive plural *gáta*, and the dative plural *gátum*, but was mutated in the dative singular and the nominative plural *gǽt*. In Middle English, the northern dialects show the normal *gāt, gait*, the southern dialects show *goot, goat*. The plural *gǽt* is represented in southern and midland dialects by *gēt, geet, geat*; the northern dialects show an unmutated form *gait* (possibly influenced by Old Norse *geitr*). A singular *geet* in the 14th century is probably the result of assimilation to the plural.

Old English *gát*, being feminine, denoted only the female goat; the male was called *bucca* BUCK *n.*[1], also *gátbucca* GOAT-BUCK. The extended sense seems to occur in early Middle English, and is frequent in the 14th century. The distinctive terms *he-goat* and *she-goat* appear about the end of that century, and are now the recognized terms for the two sexes (colloquially also *billy-goat* and *nanny-goat*). The young animal is called a KID.

1. **a.** A ruminant quadruped of the genus Capra.

The goat is indigenous to the Eastern Hemisphere, but by domestication naturalized in all parts of the world. It is especially noted for its hardy, lively and wanton nature, and its strong odour. Most of the species have hollow horns, curving backwards, and the male is usually bearded.

Occasionally used with allusion to the mention of "sheep" and "goats" in Matthew 25:32–33, as symbolical respectively of the righteous and the wicked at the Day of Judgement.

—after the Oxford English Dictionary

# Getting Your Goat
## The Gourmet Guide

by
### Patricia A. Moore
with
### Jill Charlotte Stanford

Illustrations by
### Susan Koch

evertype
2009

Published by Evertype, Cnoc Sceichín, Leac an Anfa, Cathair na Mart, Co. Mhaigh Eo, Éire. *www.evertype.com*.

A catalogue record for this book is available from the British Library.

ISBN-10 1-904808-25-5
ISBN-13 978-1-904808-25-1

Set in Electra, **Bell Gothic**, and *Gazelle* by Michael Everson.

Cover and interior illustrations by Susan Koch, *www.susankoch.com*. Cover design by Michael Everson.

The photo of the sand lily, *Leucocrinum montanum*, on page 132 was taken by John P. Kole in Pawnee Grasslands, northeastern Colorado.

Printed by LightningSource.

# Table of Contents

# Foreword

Goats have been a major source of food since time immemorial. Ancient cave paintings show the hunting of goats. They are also one of the oldest domesticated animals on earth. The scientific name for goat is Capri circus.

Moving their herds from place to place in order to find suitable forage opened up the world to early nomadic people. The herding of goats is thought to have evolved about 10,000 years ago in the mountains of Iran.

Goat milk and the cheese made from it were revered in ancient Egypt with some pharaohs supposedly having these foods placed among the other treasures in their burial chambers. Goat milk was also widely consumed by the ancient Greeks and Romans. Goat milk has remained popular throughout history and still is consumed on a more extensive basis world wide than cow's milk.

In addition to food, goats provided early man with skins to make into cloaks, their hair was woven into yarn, and was then—as it is now—a symbol of wealth. To own many goats meant you were well-off and would never face starvation.

This book contains recipes from all over the world. They are easy, many of them quick to prepare, and absolutely delicious.

Happy eating!

Patricia A. Moore
Jill Charlotte Stanford

"No! No! Don't eat me!" said the little Goat. "I am skinny and scrawny and really do not taste good at all. Please, wait for my big brother. He is tasty and juicy. He will be coming in just a minute. Please wait for him."

"You're right!" said the Troll, looking the little goat over. "You are hardly an appetizer. I would much rather have a juicy, tasty goat. You may go."

—The Three Billy Goats Gruff

# About Goat Meat

The taste of goat meat is similar to that of lamb meat; in fact, in the English-speaking islands of the Caribbean, and in some parts of Asia, particularly India, the word "mutton" is used to describe both goat and lamb meat. However, some feel that it has a similar taste to veal or venison, depending on the age and condition of the goat. It can be prepared in a variety of ways including stewed, curried, baked, grilled, barbecued, minced, canned, or made into sausage. Goat jerky is also another popular variety. In India, the rice-preparation of mutton biryani uses goat meat as its primary ingredients to produce a rich taste. "Curry goat" is a traditional West Indian dish. Goat meat is believed to make up some 80% of the total meat consumed in the world.

Goat meat, sometimes called *chevon*, is lower than lamb in fat and cholesterol, and comparable to chicken. It also has more minerals than chicken, and is lower in total and saturated fats than many other meats. One reason for the leanness is that goats do not accumulate fat deposits or "marbling" in their muscles.

Goat meat is becoming more and more popular and is appearing in more markets. This is largely because of a certain type of goat which is raised for its sweet meat and not for its milk or hair—the Boer goat.

The Boer goat is native to South Africa and has been a staple animal for the Afrikaans-speaking Boer farmers for over 500 years. The first Boer goat to come to the United States was in 1993, to a farm in Texas. Developed especially for production of a healthy, low cholesterol lean meat coupled with a fast growth rate, the Boer goat is becoming increasingly

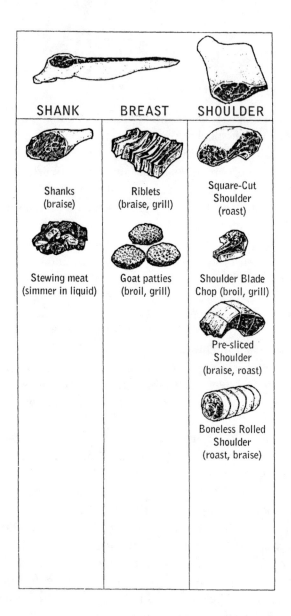

| SHANK | BREAST | SHOULDER |
|-------|--------|----------|
| Shanks (braise) | Riblets (braise, grill) | Square-Cut Shoulder (roast) |
| Stewing meat (simmer in liquid) | Goat patties (broil, grill) | Shoulder Blade Chop (broil, grill) |
| | | Pre-sliced Shoulder (braise, roast) |
| | | Boneless Rolled Shoulder (roast, braise) |

2

| RACK | LOIN | SIRLOIN | LEG |
|------|------|---------|-----|
| Rack Roast (roast) | Loin Chop (broil, grill) | Sirloin Roast (roast) | Whole Leg (roast) |
| Rib Chops (broil, grill) | Loin Roast (roast) | Sirloin Steaks (broil, grill) | Boneless Leg (oven roast, spit roast) |
| Rack for One (roast) | Double Loin Chop (broil, grill) | Sirloin Shank Half (roast) | Three-quarter French-Style Leg (roast) |
| | Medallion (broil) | Cubed Sirloin (broil, grill, stew) | Shank Half (roast) |
| | Boneless Loin (roast) | | Butterflied Leg (broil, grill) |

popular, with a wide variety of tasty recipes many of which you will find in this book.

You can find goat meat now quite readily. The list of goat meat producers is growing to meet the demand for health-conscious—as well as gourmet—food lovers. In the back of this book you will find a listing of organizations which can help you find sources for Boer meat.

Both imperial and metric measurements are given in this cookbook.

# Appetizers

*Every man can tell how many goats or sheep he possesses, but not how many friends.*

—Marcus Tullius Cicero

# Baked Goat Cheese Medallions

*8 servings*

*Quick, easy, and good!*

One 8 oz (225 g) fresh goat cheese log
2 tablespoons (30 ml) all-purpose flour
½ teaspoon (5 ml) dried basil, crushed
3 tablespoons (45 ml) melted butter
⅔ cup (80 g) chopped almonds
2–3 cups fresh, washed seedless grapes

Slice the goat cheese into ½" (1.25 cm) rounds.

Combine the flour and basil.

Dredge each cheese slice in the flour mixture.

Dip the slices into the butter, then coat each side with the chopped nuts. (Press the nuts lightly into the cheese)

Place the cheese on a plate and refrigerate about 1 hour, or until completely chilled.

Heat the oven to 400°F/200°C/Gas 6.

Place the cheese onto a baking sheet (non-stick) and bake for 6–8 minutes until the nuts are browned and the cheese is warm.

Serve the cheese with the grapes.

## *Baked Goat Cheese*   8 servings

*You will want to serve this slathered on sliced, toasted French bread or thick crackers. The flavours are amazing.*

8 oz (225 g) soft goat cheese
One 14.5 oz (410 g) can diced tomatoes, drained
¼ cup (60 ml) Kalamata olives, pitted and chopped
1 teaspoon (5 ml) chopped thyme
1 garlic clove, minced
¼ teaspoon (1.25 ml) crushed red pepper flakes
1 tablespoon (15 ml) olive oil

Preheat the oven to 350°F/180°C/Gas 4.

Place the cheese in a single layer, about 1" (2.5 cm) thick, in a 9" (22 cm) glass pie plate.

Sprinkle the tomatoes, olives, thyme, garlic, and pepper over the cheese.

Drizzle with olive oil.

Bake for 15–20 minutes.

# Brandied Goat Cheese

8 *servings*

A *perfect start to an Autumn dinner.*

8 oz (225 g) goat cheese, softened
8 oz (225 g) dairy sour cream
3 tablespoons (45 ml) brandy
1½ cups (360 ml) or 6 oz (180 g) shredded Edam
  or Gouda cheese
½ cup (60 g) walnut pieces
2 medium red apples
2 Granny Smith apples
juice of 1 lemon

Preheat the oven to 350°F/180°C/Gas 4.

In a bowl, stir together the cheese, brandy, and sour cream.
Using a spatula, pour this into an 8″ (20 cm) quiche dish or pie plate.
Bake for 45 minutes or until lightly browned.
Slice and core the apples. Sprinkle them with the lemon juice to keep them from browning.
When the cheese comes out of the oven, sprinkle with the walnut pieces.
Serve warm with the apple slices.

# Chèvre

*makes 1½–2 lbs (675–900 g)*

*French-style goat cheese is simple to make, You choose the flavour. These all freeze well in a zip-lock freezer bag.*

> 5 quarts (4.75 liters) fresh goats milk
> ½ cup (120 ml) cultured buttermilk
> 3 drops of rennet diluted in ⅓ cup (80 ml) cool water
> Cheese cloth

Warm the milk to 80°F/27°C. Stir in the buttermilk. Add the rennet/water mixture. Stir well for 60 seconds.

Cover and let stand for 8–12 hours at room temperature. When the cheese looks like thickened yoghurt, the cheese is ready to drain.

Line a large bowl with cheesecloth, leaving the edges hanging over.

Pour in the cheese (now called curds and whey) and tie the top tightly.

Hang over a bowl to drain the whey for 6–8 hours.

When it is ready, the curds roll into a good ball.

## Variations

### Dill & Garlic Chèvre

1 pound (450 g) goat cheese
1 teaspoon (5 ml) kosher sea salt
½ teaspoon (2.5 ml) garlic powder
2 teaspoons (10 ml) dill weed
2 tablespoons (30 ml) parsley flakes

Mix all ingredients well and roll the cheese and herbs into a roll. Then roll in parsley flakes.

### Chive Chèvre

As above, but substitute the garlic and dill for fresh, snipped chives

### Shrimp Chèvre

8 oz (225 g) soft goat cheese
½ cup (120 ml) sour cream
One 6 oz (180 ml) can shrimp pieces, drained

## Goat Cheese
*1 lb (450 g) of cheese*

*This is our favorite very easy, very tasty goat cheese recipe!*

**1 gallon (3.75 liters) fresh goat milk**
**¼ cup (60 ml) cider vinegar**

Heat one gallon of fresh milk to 195°F/90°C, stirring continuously to avoid scorching. Turn off heat, stir in ¼ cup (60 ml) vinegar (see notes below). Remove from heat and allow to sit for 10 minutes. The milk will coagulate into solid curd particles and clear whey. Pour the hot curds and whey into a cheesecloth lined colander, lift, and form the cheesecloth into a bag as you do. Hang it up for one hour, or until the curd has stopped dripping (you can let it hang for about an hour and a half in the shower—it sounds strange but makes cleanup so much easier!). Store in refrigerator. It's a sliceable and grateable cheese excellent for crackers and cooking.

*Tips:*

*Always* use a stainless steel pot to heat the milk and make the curds! A non-stick doesn't work very well, and anything else can actually prevent the curds from forming as they should.

*Don't* use white distilled vinegar. It doesn't work as well as apple cider vinegar. For a change of taste, experiment with things like raspberry vinegar, and so on, and you'll find it delightful. Lemon juice has been known to work as well.

*Don't* use old milk, or mix old milk and fresh milk; it won't make curds very well.

If you want to add herbs, do it after the curd has dripped for about 30 minutes, then hang it again.

For spreadable cheese, knead it a bit as you would bread dough.

For a harder, drier type of cheese, you can wring out the hanging cheese as it is dripping. It will be easier to form into a shape that fits in your storage containers.

# Goat Cheese
# & Leek Quesadillas
*8 servings*

*The only problem with this fabulous appetiser is that your guests run the risk of eating too much before the main course! Served with a crisp white wine or Sangria, these will have your guests asking for the recipe!*

2 tablespoons (30 ml) olive oil
6 cloves of garlic, chopped
1 bay leaf
1½ teaspoons (7.5 ml) dried thyme
1 large leek, washed and chopped finely
1 teaspoon (5 ml) salt
1 teaspoon (5 ml) black pepper
One 12 oz (350 ml) can artichoke hearts, drained
   and chopped
3 teaspoons (15 ml) sherry vinegar
5 oz (140 g) goat cheese, softened
1 medium tortilla
Cherry tomatoes to garnish

Heat the oil in a skillet on medium heat and sauté the garlic for 1 minute.

Add the bay leaf and thyme. Cook for an additional 2 minutes.

Add the leeks and cook until the leeks are soft.

Add the artichoke hearts and cook for 5 more minutes

Discard the bay leaf and season with the salt and pepper.

Mix with the vinegar. When cool, add the cheese and set aside.

Heat a large skillet over medium heat.

Using a paper towel, wipe the skillet with oil and add the tortilla.

Spread a heaping ½ cup (120 ml) of the artichoke mixture over the tortilla, then press with a spatula.

Brown on one side for 3 minutes.

Turn over and brown the other side.

Remove from the skillet and cut into 8 wedges. Garnish each wedge with a dollop of sour cream and a halved cherry tomato.

# Dates with Lemon Feta & Walnuts

40 appetizers

*This is a wonderful accent to have with any of the Greek-inspired goat dishes in this book. It is also a great appetiser with a hearty red wine.*

20 medjool dates, cut in half and pitted
One 7 oz (200 g) block of feta cheese
1 lemon, zested and then juiced
⅔ cup (80 g) walnut halves
Black pepper to taste
Salt to taste
Mint leaves, washed, 40

Cut the feta cheese into 40 small cubes. Place them in a small bowl and add the lemon zest and the lemon juice. Toss the cheese lightly, then add the salt and pepper.

Let stand for half an hour, stirring once.

Place one cube of cheese into each date half, then add a walnut half beside it. Season with the pepper sprinkled over the top and garnish each with a mint leaf.

# *Fruited Goat Cheese Ball*     8 *servings*

*Having a wine party or tasting? Try this wonderful cheese ball. Serve this with water crackers*

    4 oz (115 g) goat cheese, softened
    4 oz (115 g) cream cheese, softened
    2 cups (480 ml) shredded Cheddar cheese
    2 tablespoons (30 ml) honey
    2 tablespoons (30 ml) sherry
    1 teaspoon (5 ml) curry powder
    2 scallions, chopped
    ½ cup (120 ml) mixed dried fruits
    2 tablespoons (30 ml) raisins, chopped
    1 cup (240 ml) unsalted nuts, chopped

In a food processor, combine the cheeses, honey, sherry and curry. Mix until well blended.

Mix in the scallions and fruits.

Shape into a ball and roll in the chopped nuts.

Wrap tightly in plastic wrap.

Refrigerate for up to 2 days.

# Gingered Goat Cheese Ball

*8 servings*

*Elegant, pungent, and sure to be a hit.*

- 8 oz (225 g) goat cheese, softened
- 16 oz (450 g) cream cheese, softened
- 1 cup (120 ml) fresh ginger, peeled and finely chopped
- 8 oz (225 g) of salted almonds, coarsely chopped

In a food processor, combine the cheeses and ginger. Mix until blended. Shape into a ball and wrap tightly in plastic wrap.

Refrigerate overnight or up to 2 days.

Just before serving. remove the plastic wrap and roll the cheese ball in the chopped almonds until thoroughly coated.

## Goat Liver Rumaki

*6 servings*

*Rumaki is an hors d'œuvre of Polynesian origin. It was probably invented by Victor Jules Bergeron, Jr, known as "Trader" Vic. This tempting hors d'œuvre is sure to be a hit with your guests.*

> 1 lb (450 g) goat liver cut into 2″ x 2″ (5 cm x 5 cm) pieces
> One 6 oz (175 ml) can water chestnuts, sliced in half
> 8 slices bacon, cut in half
> toothpicks as needed

Wrap a slice of water chestnut around a piece of the liver. Then wrap half a bacon slice around the liver/chestnut Secure with a toothpick

Place the completed *rumaki*s on a cookie sheet and bake in a pre-heated oven at 375°F/190°C/Gas 5, for 6 minutes or until browned on one side.

Turn them over and bake the other side for an additional 4 minutes, or until browned.

Be careful not to burn them.

"Without my morning coffee I'm just like a dried up piece of roast goat."
—Johann Sebastian Bach (1685–1750)

# Roasts

"All goats are mischievous thieves, gate-crashers, and trespassers. Also they possess individual character, intelligence, and capacity for affection which can only be matched by the dog. Having once become acquainted with them I would as soon farm without a dog as without a goat."

—David Mackenzie,
Farmer in the Western Isles (1954)

# *Leg of Goat*  *8 servings*

*Nothing could be simpler—or better—than a tender leg of goat, roasted with the simplest of ingredients.*

1 leg of goat
½ cup (120 ml) lemon juice
½ cup (120 ml) cooking wine

Remove the bone from the roast, and place it in a large zip-lock bag, add lime juice and wine and marinate for 1–2 hours in lime juice and wine, turning often.

Lay the roast on a large piece of heavy duty foil.

1 tablespoon (15 ml) black pepper
1 tablespoon (15 ml) lemon pepper
1–2 tablespoons (15–30 ml) rosemary
Or add seasonings to taste.

Sprinkle both sides of the roast with seasonings. Fold the roast in half and wrap tightly with foil, adding juices from the marinate bag.

Place on a rack in a cooking pan. Bake 325°F/165°C/Gas 3 for 1 hour. Turn the oven down to 225°F/110°C/Gas ¼.

Cook on very low temperature about 4 hours. The roast will be very tender and have a delicious taste.

# Butterflied Leg of Goat    *8 servings*

*You can easily butterfly a leg by slicing down the bone and then separating the meat off the bone. Spread the meat open and you are ready to marinate it. Meat that has been marinated tastes wonderful on the grill.*

For the marinade:

> 1 cup (240 ml) dry, red wine
> ¾ cup (185 ml) soy sauce
> 4 cloves of garlic, crushed
> ½ cup (120 ml) chopped mint leaves
> 2 tablespoons (30 ml) rosemary
> 1 teaspoon (5 ml) oregano
> 1 tablespoon (15 ml) coarse pepper

Mix all these ingredients together in a large, shallow pan.

Add the butterflied pieces and marinate at least 6 hours, turning the meat twice.

Cook to medium rare on the grill.

# Sunday Leg of Goat

*6 servings*

*This is easy, flavorful, and a great Sunday dinner!*

One 3 lb (1.35 kg) leg of goat
3 garlic cloves, peeled
1 tablespoon (15 ml) paprika
½ teaspoon (2.5 ml) salt
½ teaspoon (2.5 ml) pepper
3 tablespoons (45 ml) olive oil
6 bacon slices

Wash and pat dry the leg of goat.

In a food processor, combine the garlic, paprika, salt and pepper.

Rub the leg with the olive oil, then rub the spices over it, pressing it in firmly.

Refrigerate, covered, for 2 to 3 hours to allow the marinade to work.

Remove the leg to a roasting rack. Lay the bacon over it.

Roast at 350°F/180°C/Gas 4 for 1–1½ hours, or until it is tender.

# *Pot Roast of Goat*          6 *servings*

*Comfort food, goat-meat style! Serve this with a crusty bread and a salad for a simple supper.*

One 5 lb (2.25 kg) goat shoulder
2 cups (480 ml) water
1 large onion
2 cloves garlic
Worcestershire sauce
1 teaspoon (5 ml) salt
1 teaspoon (5 ml) pepper
5 medium potatoes, halved and quartered

Preheat the oven to 300°F/150°C/Gas 2.

Put the goat meat into a roasting pot with the water. Sprinkle well with salt, pepper and Worcestershire sauce. Add chopped onion and garlic.

Bake for 5 hours. Add the potatoes ½ hour before serving.

# Goat Rack with Hazelnuts 4 servings

*There is a wonderful book written by Jill Charlotte Stanford called Lamb Country Cooking, from which this recipe has been adapted. The nutty sweet hazelnuts (sometimes called filberts) combined with the taste of goat makes a memorable dish.*

One 3 lb (1.35 kg) rack of goat
¼ cup (60 ml) vegetable oil
2 tablespoons ground hazelnuts
½ teaspoon (120 ml) salt
½ teaspoon (120 ml) pepper
⅓ cup (120 ml) chopped roasted hazelnuts*
3 dried figs, coarsely chopped

Preheat the oven to 400°F/200°C/Gas 6. Rub the rack with 2 tablespoons of oil. With fork tines, press ground hazelnuts onto the meat. Season with salt and pepper. Heat the oil in a large sauté pan until hot. Place the rack, meat side down in the pan and brown well. Turn over and place the pan in the oven for 30 to 40 minutes (until the internal temperature is 130–140°F (54–60°C) for rare to medium rare).

Remove the rack and allow it to sit for 5 minutes.

Arrange the rack in a circular fashion. Garnish the center with the chopped, roasted hazelnuts and the dried figs.

*To roast hazelnuts, chop them coarsely and put them on a baking sheet in a 350°F/180°C/Gas 4 oven for 10 minutes, stirring them once.

# Roasted Kid

*8 servings*

*Simple and flavourful. This is the best way to roast young goat (kid).*

> 1 shoulder or leg of goat, preferably kid, about 4½ pounds (2 kg)
> 3 cloves of garlic, slivered + 1 head of garlic
> 4 sprigs of rosemary
> 1 teaspoon (5 ml) fleur de sel (gourmet sea salt)
> 1 carrot, peeled and julienne sliced
> 1 onion, peeled and cut into strips
> 1 stalk of celery, peeled and cut into strips
> 1 small bouquet garni (thyme, basil, tarragon, rosemary and sage)
> 1 cup (240 ml) + 2 tablespoons (30 ml) white wine

Using a small sharp knife, make some incisions all over the kid and insert small pieces of garlic and a few rosemary leaves into each one.

Place the vegetables into a large roasting pan with the bouquet garni and head of garlic.

Place the kid on top and sprinkle with fleur de sel.

Place into a preheated 450°F/230°C/Gas 8 oven for 30 minutes.

Remove the kid from the oven and baste with the cooking juices. Return to the oven and reduce the temperature to 350°F/180°C/Gas 4. Cook for 1½ to 1¾ hours longer.

Remove the kid from the oven and let rest for 20 minutes before carving.

Deglaze the pan with the wine, scraping up the browned bits from the bottom. Bring to a boil and simmer until the liquid has reduced by two-thirds.

Correct the seasonings and strain the sauce into a sauce boat.

# How to Roast
# a Whole Cabrito
24+ servings

*This is an historical Cabrito recipe from Texas. In large Latin American communities, whole roast cabrito is the dish of choice for many celebrations.*

Cabrito is a young kid goat, 3 to 6 months of age—when it is especially tender.

The day before your celebration, dig a pit in the ground (away from trees, shrubs, and fences) deep enough and wide enough to hold the cabrito. Start a hot fire with barbecue coals. Let them burn to red-hot.

Prepare a dressed 45–60 pound (20–27 kg) kid by washing it with clear water. Rub on salt, pepper, chili powder, and cumin seed, and then cover the entire kid with a layer of lard. The lard seals in the spices and herbs. Wrap and tie meat in maguey leaves (a Mexican plant related to agave). You can also use fresh rosemary or sage branches to impart flavor.

Cover the kid with clean white sacking (old sheets work very well) and wrap it entirely in burlap that has been soaked in water, then wrung out.

Lay the covered meat on the layer of ashes over the hot coals, cover with dirt, and leave meat in the pit-ashes all night.

Another way to make whole roasted cabrito is to roast a whole kid on a spit over a slow-burning charcoal fire, turning it frequently and basting well with a barbecue sauce of your choosing to enhance the flavor.

You can eat roasted cabrito straight, fold it inside tortillas, dip it in salsa, or shred it over rice and beans.

# Shanks and Chops

*My men, like satyrs grazing on the lawns,*
*Shall with their goat feet dance an antic hay.*
*—Christopher Marlowe*

## Goat Shanks and Beans  *4 to 6 servings*

*This is a little time consuming but not labor intensive. It's a wonderful marraige of ingredients that all add up to delicious!*

1 package of 15-bean soup (discard seasoning packet)
4–6 goat leg shanks
1 large white onion
1 tablespoon (15 ml) olive oil
1 quart (1 liter) vegetable broth
¼ teaspoon (1.25 ml) salt
1 teaspoon (5 ml) pepper

The night before, cover the beans with water and soak overnight. In the morning, rinse the beans well, removing loose hulls and debris.

Preheat the oven to 400°F/200°C/Gas 6.

Put the shanks on a rack in a roasting pan, season them with the salt and pepper, then cover them with foil.

Turn the oven down to 325°F/165°C/Gas 3 and roast for 1½ hours. Do not over cook)

Dice the onion and sauté in the olive oil on low heat until they are transparent. Put the beans and onions in a slow cooker then pour the vegetable stock over them.

Cook on Low for 7 hours.

Nestle the shanks into the beans and continue cooking for an additional hour. If the beans begin to dry out, add more stock.

Serve in bowls and garnish with a dollop of sour cream or yoghurt.

# Chevon Osso Buco

*4 servings*

*Osso Buco is a northern Italian tradition. The slow cooker is the ideal way to cook this dish flavored with rosemary. Try spooning the sauce over mashed potatoes or polenta.*

4 goat shanks
2 tablespoons (30 ml) flour
¾ teaspoon (3.75 ml) black pepper
1 tablespoon (15 ml) olive oil
1 cup (240 ml) chopped carrot
1 cup (240 ml) chopped celery
1 cup (240 ml) chopped white onion
1 large garlic clove, minced
½ cup (120 ml) red wine
One 14.5 oz (430 ml) can diced tomatoes, drained
1 tablespoon (15 ml) chopped rosemary
½ teaspoon (2.5 ml) salt
1 bay leaf

Combine the flour and pepper in a shallow pan. Wash and dredge the shanks in the flour, coating them evenly.

Heat the oil in a large skillet. Add the goat shanks and braise for 2 minutes each side or until evenly browned. Place the shanks in a slow cooker.

Put all the vegetables in the pan and sauté for 5 minutes. Add the wine. Scrape the pan to loosen any browned bits. Cook over medium low heat for 1 minute.

Pour the vegetable mix over the shanks in the cooker. Add the tomatoes, rosemary, salt, and bay leaf. Stir well.

Cover and cook on Low 8–9 hours.

Discard the bay leaf before serving.

## Jamaican Jerk Goat
6 *servings*

*This authentic recipe from Jamaica adds a whole new dimension to barbecue.*

**Jerk Marinade**

6 jalapeño peppers, sliced
1 garlic clove, chopped
3 medium onions, chopped
2 tablespoons (30 ml) thyme
1 tablespooon (15 ml) sage
2 tablespoons (30 ml) allspice
2 tablespoons (30 ml) sugar
2 tablespoons (30 ml) salt
2 tablespoons (30 ml) pepper
1½ tablespoons (22.5 ml) ground cinnamon
1½ tablespoons (22.5 ml) ground ginger
1½ tablespoons (22.5 ml) ground nutmeg
1 tablespoon (15 ml) cayenne pepper
½ cup (120 ml) olive oil
½ cup (120 ml) soy sauce
1 cup (240 ml) orange juice
1 cup (240 ml) white vinegar
juice of 1 lime

Chop the onions, garlic, and peppers and put into a blender. Add the remaining ingredients, except the goat and pulse to make the jerk sauce.

Reserve ½ to 1 cup of the sauce in a covered container and refrigerate.

Cut the goat into small pieces. Use a fork to poke holes on all sides of the goat meat.

Put the meat into a large container. Add some of the sauce and rub the sauce into the meat. Add more sauce and rub again. Be sure plenty of sauce covers the meat. Cover and refrigerate overnight to marinate.

Grill the meat slowly until cooked, turning often. Baste with the reserved sauce while cooking.

Serve with reserved jerk sauce, rice (or rice and peas) and bread for an authentic Jamaican meal.

## Herbed Shanks                                    *4 servings*

*You can save washing a pan by wrapping these flavorful shanks in foil*

4 goat shanks
4 cloves of garlic, peeled and minced
1 teaspoon (5 ml) dried rosemary
1 teaspoon (5 ml) dried thyme
½ teaspoon (2.5 ml) salt
1 teaspoon (5 ml) white pepper
4 tablespoons (60 ml) tomato pureé
1 cup (240 ml) dry red wine, like Merlot

Preheat the oven to 325°F/165°C/Gas 3. Place each shank on an 18" square of heavy oven foil. Put a minced garlic clove over each, then sprinkle the remaining herbs and seasonings over them.

Shape the foil around the shanks, leaving the top open. Pour 1 tablespoon of tomato puree over each shank, then pour ¼ cup (60 ml) of wine into the foil packet. Seal the packets tightly.

Put the packets in a baking dish and bake for two hours, or until very tender.

# *Mshikaki*

8 *servings*

*Mshikaki is a popular skwered grilled meat prevalent throughout Kenya. In the capitol, Mombasa, mshikaki stands are on every corner, and each has a different taste. You can create your own by adding or subtracting the spices and herbs.*

> 3 lbs (1.5 kg) goat meat cut into 1" (2.5 cm) cubes
> ½ cup (120 ml) olive oil
> 1 cup (240 ml) yoghurt
> ½–1 teaspoon (2.5–5 ml) coriander
> 2 or 3 limes
> 1 tablespoon (15 ml) cayenne pepper
> 3 or 4 cloves garlic

Place the meat in large ceramic bowl.

Squeeze the limes and pour the juice, yoghurt, and olive oil into a blender. Mince the garlic and add to the liquid along with coriander and cayenne pepper.

Blend the marinade for one minute. Pour it over the meat in the large bowl. Cover and set aside for 2 to 3 hours.

Skewer the meat and sear it over a hot grill for 15 minutes, basting with remaining marinade.

Good served with chunks of fresh mango and a tangy salad.

## Oven Barbecue Spareribs        4 servings

*Michelle Jackson-Hirsch lives in Colorado Springs, Colorado. She loves computers and cooking and especially this recipe.*

Preheat the oven to 350°F/180°C/Gas 4.

1 lb (450 g) goat ribs
2 tablespoons (30 ml) olive oil
2 cloves of garlic, minced
1 cup (240 ml) catsup
⅔ cup (160 ml) chili sauce
2 tablespoons (30 ml) prepared mustard
¼ cup (60 ml) brown sugar
½ cup (120 ml) onion, chopped
2 tablespoons (30 ml) Worcestershire sauce
2 teaspoons (10 ml) celery seed
½ teaspoon (2.5 ml) salt
1 lemon, sliced thinly

Cut the ribs into serving size pieces—at least two ribs per person.

Put these in a saucepan and cover them with salted water. Bring to a boil, then lower the heat. Cover and simmer for 1–2 hours or until tender.

Heat the olive oil in a skillet and add the garlic. Sauté for 5 minutes. Add the remaining ingredients and bring to a boil

Drain the ribs and place them in a shallow baking pan.

Pour the sauce over the ribs and bake, (covered) in the preheated oven for 1 hour, basting often.

# Wine-Braised Goat Shanks    *4 servings*
*Slow cooked goat shanks in a red wine sauce.*

4 goat shanks
1 tablespoon (15 ml) black pepper
5 basil leaves, torn
1 tablespoon (15 ml) salt
⅓ cup (80 ml) extra virgin olive oil
juice of 2 lemons
4 cloves garlic, peeled and chopped
2 raw medium onions, peeled and sliced thinly
One 15 oz (425 g) can diced tomatoes
2 cups (480 ml) burgundy wine
1 tablespoon (15 ml) balsamic vinegar
1 cup (240 ml) brown sugar, packed

Preheat oven to 275°F/140°C/Gas 1.

Layer onions on the bottom of a lidded pan. Place shanks on top. Pour wine, balsamic vinegar, and olice oil over shanks. Sprinkle brown sugar on top. Place cloves of garlic and lemon wedges between the shanks. Pour tomatoes over the top, then sprinkle the salt, pepper, and basil on top.

Cover and bake for 3 hours.

Alternatively, cook in a slow cooker on High for 4 hours.

Serve immediately.

# Sate Kambing
*4 servings*

*This coconut goat satay is a favorite on the island of Java in Indonesia.*

4 goat leg chops
1 small onion
1 clove of garlic, peeled and crushed
1 tablespoon (15 ml) tamarind sauce
1 tablespoon (15 ml) light soy sauce
1 tablespoon (15 ml) vinegar
1 teaspoon (5 ml) *sambal ulek* (see the recipe on the next page)
1 cup (240 ml) shredded coconut
2 tablespoons (30 ml) vegetable oil
1 teaspoon (5 ml) Sesame oil

Trim the bones from the goat chops and cut them into ¾″ (2 cm) cubes.

Combine the goat with chopped onion, garlic, tamarind sauce, soy sauce, vinegar, *sambal ulek* and coconut. Marinate for 2 hours or refrigerate overnight.

Thread the goat onto squewers and brush with combined the oils.

Cook under a hot preheated grill for 3 minutes.

# Sambal ulek
*1 batch*

*A staple in Malaysian and Thai cooking.* **Ulek** *means "grinding" so* **sambal ulek** *means 'ground chili paste'! This can also be frozen. To make one batch:*

1 lb (450 g) red chilies
5½ oz (160 g) garlic, peeled and chopped
5½ oz (160 g) tender young ginger, peeled and
   chopped
2 stalks lemon grass, thinly sliced (white part only)
6 fluid oz (180 ml) vinegar
8 oz (225 g) sugar
salt to taste
1 tablespoon (15 ml) lime zest, chopped

Blend the chilies, garlic, ginger and lemon grass in a food processor While processing gradually add the vinegar.

Place the pureed mixture into a saucepan and bring to a boil. Reduce the heat and simmer for 3 minutes.

Add the sugar and stir until dissolved. Add the salt and lime zest.

Remove from the heat, cool and bottle in sterilized jars.

## Sweet & Sour Goat Shanks     4 servings

*Slow cooking in a rich sauce on a bed of onion rings makes these shanks a recipe favorite! This is good served with mashed Yukon Gold potatoes on the side, spooning the onions and gravy over the potatoes.*

4 goat shanks.
2 tablespoons (30 ml) flour
⅔ cup (160 ml) olive oil, divided
1 tablespoon (15 ml) fresh ground black pepper
1 tablespoon (15 ml) salt
1 medium sweet white onion
1 cup (240 ml) brown sugar
1 tablespoon (15 ml) balsamic vinegar
2 medium lemons, cut into fourths
One 15 oz (440 g) can diced tomatoes,
1 teaspoon (5 ml) ground basil
1 teaspoon (5 ml) ground oregano

Preheat oven to 275°F/140°C/Gas 1.

Roll the shanks in the flour. Heat ⅓ cup of the oil in a skillet and brown the shanks on all sides. Season with the salt and pepper

In a large, lidded casserole, heat the remaining oil. Slice the onion thinly and sauté until transparent, stirring frequently.

Place shanks on top of the onion. Sprinkle brown sugar on top. Add the Balsamic vinegar. Squeeze the lemons over the top and put the rinds in.

Add the tomatoes and the herbs.

Cover and bake for 3 hours in the oven.

If you are using a slow cooker, set the timer for 6 hours on medium-low

## Barbecued Goat          *6 servings*

*This can be made with shanks, ribs, chops, or steaks. Finger-licking good!*

5 lb (2.25 kg) goat meat
½ cup (120 ml) prepared mustard
½ cup (120 ml) lemon pepper
½ cup (120 ml) chili powder
2 tablespoons (30 ml) garlic, crushed
1 teaspoon (5 ml) cayenne pepper

Sauce:
1 cup (240 ml) butter
5 large garlic cloves peeled, crushed
2 large bay leaves
3 large lemon quartered
1 large lime quartered
1 medium onion sliced
12 oz (350 ml) beer
2 cups (480 ml) corn oil
½ cup (120 ml) Worcestershire sauce
2 tablespoons (30 ml) chili powder
½ teaspoon (2.5 ml) cayenne pepper

Rub the meat completely with the mustard. Mix the spices together well. Coat the meat with the spice rub, cover and refrigerate overnight.

In a 2 quart (2 liter) saucepan melt the butter, add the onions and garlic. Sauté for 5 minutes then add the lemons, limes and beer.

When the foam subsides add the remaining ingredients and simmer for 20–25 minutes.

Prepare the grill for the indirect heat method and remove the meat from the fridge and place on the grill.

Smoke for 25 minutes at 250°F/130°C and start basting with the sauce every 25 minutes.

Smoke for 2–3 hours or until the internal temperature reaches 155°F/70°C, then wrap in foil and finish cooking until the internal temperature reaches 185°F/85°C. Remove from the grill and let the meat cool for 20 minutes prior to slicing.

## Rosemary Goat Shanks          *6 servings*

*"Rosemary for Remembrance". No one will forget these delicious and moist goat shanks. A crusty loaf of bread goes well with this dish, to soak up the flavourful juices.*

6 goat shanks
6 large sweet onions
6 tablespoons (90 ml) olive oil
1 teaspoon (5 ml) salt
1½ teaspoons (7.5 ml) pepper
1 teaspoon (5 ml) dried rosemary
1 teaspoon (5 ml) thyme
1 bay leaf, torn into pieces
2½ cups (600 ml) chicken or vegetable broth

Heat 2 tablespoons (30 ml) of the oil in a heavy skillet.
Brown the shanks on all sides.
Season with the salt, the pepper and rosemary.
Remove from the pan.
Heat the remaining oil and sauté the onion until transparent.
Transfer the onions to a heavy casserole dish. Lay the shanks on top.
Add the thyme, and the bay leaf, then pour the broth over all.
Bake, uncovered, at 350°F/180°C/Gas 4 for 2–2½ hours, or until tender.
Before serving, remove the bay leaf pieces.

# Soups, Stews, and Casseroles

# Getting Your Goat

*And if his offering be a goat, then he shall offer it before the Lord.*

*—Leviticus 3:12*

# Chevon Moroccan

*6 servings*

*Cat Addison is a go-get 'em kind of gal. She loves new adventures and especially new recipes. She says, "Chevon Moroccan was my first taste of goat meat. It is now one of my favorite dishes and I have prepared it for others to get them to see how wonderful goat meat is too."*

3 tablespoons (45 ml) olive oil
2 lb (900 g) goat meat, cubed in 1" (2.5 cm) pieces
½ lb (225 kg) fresh, sliced mushrooms
1½ onions, chopped
1 garlic clove, minced
1 lb (450 g) fresh tomatoes, peeled and quartered
½ cup (120 ml) raisins
½ cup (120 ml) toasted almond slices
2 tablespoons (30 ml) sugar
1 teaspoon (5 ml) cinnamon
1 teaspoon (5 ml) salt
¼ teaspoon (1.25 ml) allspice
¼ cup (60 ml) chicken broth

Heat the oil in a large skillet. Add the goat meat and sauté until browned. Add the mushrooms, onions and garlic. Sauté for 2 more minutes.

Add the tomatoes, raisins, almonds, sugar, cinnamon, salt and allspice.

Add the broth and simmer for one hour, stirring occasionally, until the meat is tender. Add more broth if needed as it simmers.

Serve the stew over couscous for a truly authentic dish.

# African Goat Soup

6 servings

*Goats are a symbol of a family's wealth in Africa. The more goats they have, the wealthier they are. Too many goats? They serve them up in this tasty soup which is more like a stew. Serve it with a good loaf of crusty bread and a bottle of hearty red wine.*

2 lbs (900 g) lean goat meat, cut into 1" (2.5 cm) cubes
¼ cup (60 ml) of flour
3 tablespoons (45 ml) olive oil
1 large yellow onion, sliced
1 cup (240 ml) celery, cut into pieces
1½ cups (360 ml) carrots, cut into pieces
2 cups (480 ml) sweet potatoes (or yams) washed, skinned, and cubed
3 cups (710 ml) vegetable broth
1 cup (240 ml) water
¼ cup (60 ml) white wine (optional) salt and pepper to taste
1 clove garlic, mashed
1 teaspoon (5 ml) cinnamon
1 tablespoon (15 ml) cumin

Trim any excess fat from the meat. Dredge the meat in the flour that has the salt and pepper added to it. Coat it well.

In a heavy skillet, put 1 tablespoon of the olive oil and saute the meat until browned on all sides. Remove from the pan.

Add the remaining olive oil and saute the vegetables until the onions are clear.

Put the meat back into the pan and add the vegetable broth, white wine, water and spices.

You may also put everything into a Slow Cooker .

Simmer, covered, for 5 or 6 hours on Low, stirring occassionally.

# Cabrito en Mole Verde Picante

*4 servings*

*Mole is the generic name for several sauces used in Mexican cuisine. This one is a spicy green sauce, to be served with the meat of a young goat, from Jim and Terrie Gattey of Bend, Oregon.*

- 1 lb (450 g) goat leg meat, cut into 1″ (2.5 cm) cubes
- ¼ cup (60 ml) flour
- 1½ teaspoons (7.5 ml) salt
- 2 teaspoons (10 ml) dried oregano
- 3 tablespoons (45 ml) vegetable oil, divided
- 6 medium tomatillos, husked, roasted and chopped
- 2 medium fresh pasilla chilies, charred over an open flame or under the broiler until the skin is blackened on all sides, peeled, stemmed, seeded and chopped
- 1 large fresh jalapeño chili, prepared as above
- 3 medium fresh serrano chilies, prepared as above
- 1 medium yellow onion, peeled, sliced and coarsely chopped
- 4 garlic cloves, peeled and sliced
- One 14 oz (415 ml) can of beef broth
- One 12 oz (350 ml) bottle of medium to dark beer

In a large skillet or Dutch oven, heat half the oil.

Mix the salt, pepper and oregano in a bowl and toss the goat meat in the mix. Dredge the seasoned meat in the flour and brown on all sides in the oil. Remove from the pan.

Reduce the heat in the pan, and deglaze with a splash of beer to loosen any small bits of meat. Add the remaining oil and add the onion, garlic, and tomatillos. Sauté until soft.

Add the chilies and sauté for about eight minutes.

Add the beef broth, the remaining beer and hear for five minutes.

Return the goat meat to the pan, reduce the heat to simmer and cook for 20 minutes.

Serve with fresh flour tortillas. Provide garnishes of chopped peeled tomatoes, fresh cilantro, and diced avacados, as well as a dollop of sour cream.

## Chevon Casserole

*6 servings*

*A lovely spring casserole. The taste of dill, along with fresh tomatoes makes this a favorite.*

  1½ lb (680 g) ground goat
  1 cup (240 ml) chopped fresh dill weed
  4 lbs (1.8 kg) potatoes skinned and cubed into ½″
    (1.25 cm) cubes
  1 large onion, chopped
  1 cup (240 ml) olive oil
  6 eggs
  ½ cup (120 ml) chopped parsley
  1 teaspoon (5 ml) salt
  1 teaspoon (5 ml) pepper
  2 fresh tomatoes, diced
  1 cup (240 ml) Parmesan cheese
  ½ cup (120 ml) butter, melted

Preheat the oven to 350°F/180°C/Gas 4.

Boil the potatoes in salted water until tender. Drain them, and mash thoroughly, then set aside. Once they have cooled, add 4 eggs of the eggs, the dill weed and half of the Parmesan cheese. Mix well.

In a large skillet, heat the oil and brown the ground meat with the onions. Add the tomatoes, parsley and salt and pepper. Cook and stir the mixture for 15 minutes then set it aside. Once it has cooled, add two eggs and mix it all together.

Butter a large baking dish. Smooth half of the potato mixture over the bottom then smooth the goat mixture and top it off with the remaining potatoes.

Pour the melted butter over the casserole and sprinkle the remaining cheese over it. Bake it for 40 minutes.

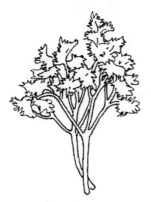

# Braised Goat Stroganoff
## for the slow cooker *4 servings*

*Marilyn Manfrine Burke offers this tasty and quick, not to mention easy, recipe. Serve this over thin fettucine or egg noodles. Some braised asparagus or brussels sprouts would be perfect on the side.*

> 2 lb (900 g) goat meat, cubed
> 1 cup (240 ml) sour cream
> One 16 oz (450 g) can of tomato sauce
> 1 clove garlic, peeled and minced
> ½ cup (120 ml) chopped sweet onion
> 1¼ tablespoons (20 ml) paprika
> 1 teaspoon (5 ml) salt
> ½ teaspoon (2.5 ml) pepper
> 1 teaspoon (5 ml) Worcestershire sauce

Mix all these ingredients together in the slow cooker and cook on Low for 6 to 8 hours, or High 4 to 5 hours.

Serve over rice or cooked noodles.

# Sauerkraut Goat

*4 servings*

*This pungent recipe comes from Germany, where goat is often consumed. Even if you are not a fan of sauerkraut, try this—it is excellent and it might change your mind. about an often overlooked pickled condiment.*

> 5 lb (2.25 kg) shank half of goat
> Two 14 oz (400 g) cans of sauerkraut
> 2 medium onions. sliced
> 2 tablespoons (30 ml) minced garlic
> 4 tablespoons (60 ml) Worcestershire sauce
> 2 teaspoons (10 ml) salt
> 1 teaspoon (5 ml) pepper

Put the meat in roasting pan. Spread the contents of the first can of sauerkraut (with juice) around the meat; spread the contents of the second can on top of the meat.

Slice the onions and put on top of the meat.

Sprinkle garlic, salt, pepper and Worcestershire sauce on top.

Cover with foil and bake at 300°F/150°C/Gas 2, basting several times with the juices during cooking.

Cook for 4 hours or until the meat falls off the bone.

## Curried Cabrito

*6 servings*

*Spicy and full of the taste of India.*

3 lb (1.4 kg) goat meat
2 tablespoons (30 ml) cardamon
2–3 cloves
2–3 cinnamon sticks
3–4 bay leaves
1 teaspoon (5 ml) whole black pepper
¼ cup (60 ml) oil
4 chopped onions
2 chopped tomatoes
2 tablespoons (30 ml) tomato puree
1 tablespoon (15 ml) garlic paste
1 tablespoon (15 ml) ginger paste
2 tablespoons (30 ml) chopped fresh coriander leaves
1 tablespoon (15 ml) red chili powder
1 tablespoon (15 ml) coriander powder
1 teaspoon (5 ml) turmeric powder
1 tablespoon (15 ml) garam masala
Salt to taste
Water for gravy (curry)

Heat the oil in the frying pan, add cardamon, cloves, cinnamon stick, bay leaves, whole black pepper and sauté for few seconds. Then add the onions and sauté until light brown. Add ginger garlic paste, tomato, tomato puree, coriander powder, red chili, turmeric, and salt to taste. When the masala is thoroughly sautéd and the oil comes up add the cabrito pieces and sauté until brown. Then add water, cover the pan and keep it on a low flame until the cabrito is done. Garnish with chopped coriander (cilantro) leaves and garam masala for a delicious flavor. Serve with roti or naan bread.

# Egyptian Goat Casserole    6 servings

*A simple casserole to eat as you float down the Nile on your Royal Barge.*

> 1 pound of goat meat, cut into 1" (2.5 cm) cubes
> ⅛ cup cider vinegar
> One 6 oz (180 ml) can tomato paste
> 2 tomatoes, chopped coarsely
> ½ tablespoon salt
> ½ tablespoon pepper
> 5 medium white potatoes, peeled and sliced into ¼"
>    slices
> 3 large white onions, peeled and sliced into ¼" rings
> cooking spray

Place the goat meat into a large bowl. Cover with cold water and add ⅛ cup of vinegar. Marinate for 1 hour, turning the meat several times.

Pour off the vinegar and rinse the meat in cool water. Put the meat in a cooking pot and add enough water to cover. Bring to a boil and boil on medium heat for 15 minutes.

Turn off the heat. Do not drain.

Put the tomato paste into the pot. Stir it to dissolve. Add the tomatoes, salt and pepper.

Place the potatoes and onions in another cooking pot. Cover with water and bring to a boil. Cook for about 7 minutes or until the potatoes are tender. Remove from the heat but do not drain.

Coat a large casserole with cooking spray. Using a slotted spoon, put about ⅓ of the goat/tomato mixture into the dish. Spread evenly. Top with a layer of the potato and onions. Repeat, with a layer of goat and tomato on top.

Bake uncovered at 375°F/190°C/Gas 5 for approximately 2 hours, or until very tender.

You can add the potato water if it begins to dry out.

# Goat Daube Provençal

6 *servings*

*This is a twist on the classic French braised meat, red wine and vegetable stew. This is wonderful served over egg noodles.*

2 teaspoons (10 ml) olive oil
12 garlic cloves, crushed
2 lbs (900 g) of goat meat, cut into 1" cubes
1½ teaspoons (7.5 ml) salt, divided
½ teaspoon (2.5 ml) black pepper, divided
1 cup (240 ml) red wine
2½ cups (600 ml) baby carrots
1½ cups (350 ml) chopped sweet onion
½ cup (120 ml) beef broth
1 tablespoon (15 ml) tomato paste
1 teaspoon (5 ml) fresh rosemary, chopped
1 teaspoon (5 ml) fresh thyme, chopped
⅛ teaspoon (1 ml) ground cloves
One 14½ oz (430 ml) can diced tomatoes
1 bay leaf

In a large skillet, heat the oil over low heat. Add the garlic and cook for 5 minutes or until the garlic is tender, stirring occasionally. Remove the garlic with a slotted spoon and set aside.

Increase the heat to medium-high. Add the goat meat to the pan and sprinkle it with ½ teaspoon of the salt and ¼ teaspoon of the pepper. Braise for 5 minutes, browning on all sides. Remove the meat from the pan.

Add the wine to the pan. Bring to a boil, scraping up the browned bits.

Add the garlic, goat meat carrots,onions, tomato paste, broth, herbs and seasonings and the remaining salt and pepper.

Bring to a boil.

Place this all into a slow cooker. Cover and cook on High for 5 hours.

Or, place in an ovenproof casserole and bake, covered, at 350°F/180°C/Gas 4 for 5 hours.

# Greek Goat Stew

*4 servings*

*Goats are wealth to the Greeks. They have depended on goats for food for centuries. Save some of the wine for the cooking for your glass for a toast!*

2 lb (900 g) boneless goat, cubed
2 medium onions, chopped
3 tablespoons (45 ml) butter
1 garlic clove, minced
1 tablespoon (15 ml) chopped parsley
One 6 oz (180 ml) can tomato paste
2 cups (480 ml) water
1 cup (240 ml) white wine
salt and pepper

Melt the butter in a stew pan or Dutch oven; add the meat, onion, garlic, parsley, salt and pepper; brown over medium heat, stirring constantly. The gentle braising of the meat is the secret to success with this recipe.

When all of the ingredients are delicately browned, add tomato paste diluted in 2 cups water; add wine; stir; lower the heat and simmer for about 1½ hours.

This goat stew is the basis for a wide variety of combinations with fresh or frozen vegetables.

Potatoes: Wash and peel 12 small potatoes, brown them lightly in butter, and add to stew. Simmer until the potatoes are tender and sprinkle with chopped parsley before serving. Almost any other vegetable can be added to the basic recipe.

## Jamaican Curried Goat
*6 servings*

*Denise Wallace lived in Jamaica and sends along this delicious recipe from her home in Bend, Oregon.*

2 lb (900 g) goat meat, cubed
1 tablespoon (15 ml) curry powder
2 onions, peeled and diced
2 scallions, peeled and diced
½ teaspoon (2.5 ml) salt
½ teaspoon (2.5 ml) pepper
2 fresh jalapeño peppers, deseeded and chopped
1 tablespoon (15 ml) fresh ginger, grated
2 springs of fresh thyme
6 cloves of garlic, peeled and minced
½ cup (120 ml) of water
1 cup (240 ml) carrots, diced
1 cup (240 ml) potatoes, diced
1 tablespoon (15 ml) butter

Combine the curry powder, onions, scallions, salt, pepper, jalapenos, ginger, thyme, garlic and water in a food processor or blender. Pulse. Add more water if the ingredients "stick".

Run the marinade into the cubes of meat. Store in a covered container overnight in the refrigerator.

Remove the meat from the marinade and take off as much of the marinade as possible. Melt the butter in a frying pan, add the meat, and brown gently.

Place the meat in a 4-6 quart stock pot. Add the carrots, potatoes and the marinade. Add enough water to just cover the meat.

Bring to a boil and turn the heat to simmer. Simmer until the meat is tender, about 1–1½ hours.

Serve with rice and peas.

# *Middle Eastern Goat*     6 *servings*

The secret—your secret—to this wonderul dish from the middle east is using a suprising blend of herbs and spices: cardamom, tumeric and coriander. Cardamom has a strong, unique taste, with an intensely aromatic fragrance. Tumeric has an earthy, peppery flavor and a mustardy smell, while cardamom is the seed of the cilantro plant.

> 1 lb (450 g) boneless goat cut into 1″ (2.5 cm) pieces
> 1 tablespoon (15 ml) cardamom powder
> 1 tablespoon (15 ml) turmeric powder
> 1 tablespoon (15 ml) black pepper, ground
> 1 tablespoon (15 ml) coriander powder
>
> For the paste:
> ½ cup (120 ml) of olive oil
> 8 oz (225 g) plain yoghurt, whisked
> 4 tomatoes, finely chopped
> 1 tablespoon (15 ml) cardamom powder
> 1 tablespoon (15 ml) turmeric powder
> 1 tablespoon (15 ml) black pepper, ground
> 1 tablespoon (15 ml) coriander powder

Combine all the herbs and spices and add enough water to make a paste—about 5–6 tablespoon (75–90 ml).

Heat oil in a pot or wok. Add cardamom paste and ground pepper, and sauté on low heat for 2–3 minutes.

Add the meat, and turn it well, making sure all the pieces are coated with the paste.

Add the turmeric and coriander powders, and turn the meat to coat all the pieces with the spices.

Sauté the meat in the spices for a full 10 minutes, still on low heat. Turn constantly, to ensure the spices don't burn and that the meat doesn't stick to the bottom of the pot.

Still in low heat, add the yoghurt, tomatoes and salt to taste. Sauté for another 5 minutes.

Add 1 pint (500 ml) of hot water, bring to a boil and then lower the heat. Cover the pot and simmer until the meat is tender, about 45–60 minutes.

Garnish with chopped coriander.

Serve with steamed rice or naan bread.

## Nigerian Goat Stew

6 *servings*

*Bolu Tunrarebi sends this from Nigeria.*

2½ lb (1.13 kg) of boneless goat meat, cubed
1 teaspoon (5 ml) thyme
1 teaspoon (5 ml) curry powder
2 onions, peeled and sliced
5 or 6 fresh jalapeño peppers, seeded and chopped
2 cups (480 ml) of tomatoes, sliced
2 cloves of garlic, peeled and crushed
1 cup (240 ml) tomato purée
2 teaspoons (10 ml) fresh basil
⅔ cup (160 ml) vegetable stock
¼ cup (60 ml) peanut oil
Salt to taste

Heat some of the oil in a 6 quart (5.5 liter) pot. Season the goat meat with salt and then to the pot along with the onions, thyme and curry powder. Cook for 30–35 minutes, stirring frequently.

In a food processor or blender combine the onions, jalapenos and tomatoes, Pulse to a coarse consistency.

Heat the reaming oil in a separate skillet. Add the tomato blend and garlic and sauté for 20 minutes until fairly dry.

Add this mixture, along with the tomato paste and stock to the goat pieces. Stir thoroughly.

Bring to a boil. Add the basil and then simmer for 10 minutes, stirring frequently. Drain off any oil that rises to the surface.

Serve with boiled rice or fried plantains.

# Simple Goat Stroganoff

6 servings

*Susan Conner is a retired large-animal veterinarian who lives in Sisters, Oregon. Now she raises a few goats, rides and drives her horses, and enjoys her 10-acre mini farm. All this keeps her busy, so she does not have much time to cook—but this recipe is fast and simple!*

2 lb (900 g) goat meat, cubed
2 tablespoons (30 ml) olive oil
1 clove of minced garlic
2 14 oz (415 ml) cans of onion soup, undiluted
1½ cups (360 ml) of sour cream
1 cup (240 ml) of fresh sliced mushrooms

Brown the meat in the olive oil and season it with the salt and pepper.

Place in a casserole dish. Add the onion soup, mushrooms and garlic.

Bake in a preheated 350°F/180°C/Gas 4 oven for one hour.

Stir in the sour cream and serve over cooked rice or noodles.

# ¡Olé! Goat Chili
8 *servings*

*A taste of Mexico, goat style! A wonderful combination of herbs and spices make this a winner.*

2 lb (900 g) goat meat, cut very coarsely
2 cups (480 ml) white onion, chopped
2 cloves of garlic, minced
2 teaspoons (10 ml) cumin
½ teaspoon (2.5 ml) oregano
1 teaspoon (5 ml) coriander
Two 4.5 oz (133 ml) cans of green chilies, chopped
Three 15.5 oz (460 ml) cans cannellini beans, rinsed
    and drained
One 14 oz (415 ml) can chicken broth
1 tablespoon (15 ml) chili powder
1 cup (240 ml) Monterey Jack cheese, shredded
½ cup (120 ml) fresh cilantro, chopped
½ cup (120 ml) green onion, chopped

Heat a skillet over medium-high heat. Coat the pan with cooking spray.

Add the goat meat to the pan and cook, stirring, for 10 minutes, or until browned.

Heat a large cooking pot over medium-high heat. Coat the pan with cooking spray. Add the onion, cilantro and chili powder. Sauté until the onion is transparent. Add the garlic. Stir in the cumin, oregano and coriander and sauté for 1 minute.

Stir in the chilies and reduce the heat to low*. Cook for 1 hour, partially covered.

Add the goat meat, beans and broth and bring to a simmer. Simmer for 10 minutes, stirring occasionally. Stir in the hot sauce.

Serve in bowls and top with the cheese and green onion.

* You can cook this in your slow cooker on Low for 6 hours at this point.

## Slow-cooker Goat Stew          6 servings

*The addition of beer makes this an unforgettable stew!*

2 cups (480 ml) cubed and peeled red potatoes
2 cups (480 ml) baby carrots
2 cups (480 ml) cremini mushrooms, quartered
1 cup (240 ml) onion, chopped
1 cup (240 ml) celery, chopped
½ cup (120 ml) tomato paste
2 teaspoons (10 ml) sugar
2 teaspoons (10 ml) oregano
1½ teaspoons (7.5 ml) thyme
1 teaspoon (5 ml) rosemary
¾ teaspoon (3.75 ml) black pepper
½ teaspoon (2.5 ml) salt
3 large cloves
2 bay leaves

½ cup (120 ml) flour
¼ teaspoon (1.25 ml) salt
¼ teaspoon (1.25 ml) pepper
1 lb (450 g) goat stew meat
1 tablespoon (15 ml) olive oil

1 cup (240 ml) dark brown beer
One 14 oz (415 ml) can of beef broth

Combine the first 14 ingredients in an electric slow cooker.
Combine the flour, salt and pepper in a shallow dish.
Dredge the goat meat in the flour mixture.

Heat the oil in a large non stick skillet over medium high
heat. Add the goat and cook until browned on all sides.

Add the goat meat to the vegtables and herbs in the cooker.
Pour the beer and the broth over it all.

Cover and cook on Low about 7 hours or until the meat is
tender.

## Birria
*8 servings*

Birria (accent on the first syllable) is a spicy Mexican meat stew. Originally from Jalisco, it is a common dish in some Mexican food establishments and it is sold by street vendors. It is served with corn tortillas, onion, cilantro, and lime.

Birria is made using a base of dried roasted peppers. This gives birria both its characteristic savouriness as well as its remarkable variety, as different cooks will choose different peppers to use for the broth base. Birria is served by combining a bowl of broth with freshly chopped roasted meat of the customer's choice. One eats it by filling a corn tortilla with meat, onions and cilantro, seasoning with fresh squeezed lime juice, and then dipping it into the broth before eating it. The broth itself is also eaten with a spoon or by drinking from the bowl. This authentic recipe is from Asminda Zavala.

5 lb (2.25 kg) goat meat with bone
3 heads of garlic
16 bay leaves
3 tablespoons (45 ml) thyme
3 tablespoons (45 ml) marjoram
1½ medium onions, peeled
6 tablespoons (90 ml) salt
18 guajillo chilies
5 puya chilies

Toast all the chilies on a hot pan until they are browned but not burned. Then remove the seeds and veins. Boil them until they are soft. Drain the water and put them in a blender with one garlic head, half of an onion, 8 of the bay leaves, 3 tablespoons (45 ml) of the thyme, 3 tablespoons (45 ml) of the marjoram, 4 tablespoons (60 ml) of salt. Blend until it is all smooth. Put this mixture through a small screen colander to get rid of the small pieces left in the liquid.

Marinate the meat in this sauce for a minimum of 3 hours —overnight is better.

Add 3 cups of water to a Dutch oven. Add the remaining onion cut into pieces, the remaining garlic (2 heads) the remaining bay leaves and the remaining salt. Put in the meat.

Gently boil for 3 hours on medium heat. Check for tenderness after two hours.

Serve with corn tortilla tacos with red sauce, chopped onions, cilantro, and a bit of lime—or with beans, Spanish rice, and salsa.

# Irish Stewed Goat & Potatoes
*8 servings*

*From Ireland comes this dish. Instead of lamb, many crofters are turning to goat for their meat as well as for the milk. (See An Irish Ice Cream Secret on page 117.)*

5 lb (2.25 kg) goat shoulder
2 cups (480 ml) water
1 large onion
2 cloves garlic
Worcestershire sauce
salt
pepper
5 medium potatoes

Put goat meat into roasting pot with water. Sprinkle well with salt, pepper and Worcestershire sauce. Add chopped onion and garlic. Put on lowest heat on stove. Cook for 5 hours. Add potatoes ½ hour before serving.

# Thai-style Chevon Stew

8 *servings*

*Peanut butter makes an appearance and lends the taste to this dish fit for "The King and I".*

2 lb (900 g) goat meat, cut into stew-size pieces
2 cups (480 ml) red bell pepper, seeded and sliced thinly
¼ cup (60 ml) teriyaki sauce
2 tablespoons (30 ml) rice vinegar
1 teaspoon (5 ml) crushed red pepper flakes
2 garlic cloves, minced
¼ cup (60 ml) creamy peanut butter
6 cups (1.4 liters) cooked and hot basmati rice
½ cup (120 ml) green onions, chopped
2 tablespoons (30 ml) dry-roasted peanuts, chopped
8 lime wedges

Place the goat meat, bell pepper, teriyaki sauce, rice vinegar and red pepper into a 4 quart (4 liter) electric slow cooker. Cover and cook on High for 1 hour. Reduce the heat to Low and cook for 6 hours.

Add the peanut butter and stir well.

Serve this stew over the rice in individual bowls.

Top with the onions and peanuts.

Serve with lime wedges on the side.

# Thai Curry Goat Stew          6 servings

*This Thai-inspired recipe combines aromatic and bold herbs and spices. We would pair this with a hearty Syrah wine.*

¼ cup (60 ml) packed, fresh basil leaves
3 tablespoons (45 ml) fresh, peeled chopped ginger
3 tablespoons (45 ml) lime juice
1 tablespoon (15 ml) Thai seasoning
2 teaspoons (10 ml) curry powder
1 teaspoon (5 ml) dried lemon grass
3 shallots, peeled and halved

1½ lb (680 g) boneless leg of goat, trimmed and cut
    into 1" (2.5 cm) cubes

2½ cups (600 ml) peeled and cubed Yukon Gold
    potatoes
2 tablespoons (30 ml) fish sauce
One 14.5 oz (430 ml) can diced tomatoes, undrained
One 14 oz (415 ml) can light coconut milk
Fresh ground black pepper

Place the first 7 ingredients in a food processor and pulse until a paste forms. Spoon this in to a 4 quart (4 liter) slow cooker.

Add the goat and the next four ingredients. Stir well.

Cover and cook on High for 1 hour,

Reduce the heat to Low and cook for 7 hours or until the goat meat is tender.

Ladle into individual bowls. Sprinkle with pepper.

# Ground Goat

*If the beards were all, goats could preach.*
　　　　　　　　　　　—Danish proverb

## Chevon Vegetable Pie
*6 servings*

*This is a perfect dish for a winter's night. Susan Conner says,"I have used a variety of cheeses, such as Parmesan, Mozzarella, a Mozzarella Cheddar blend, goat cheese and Soy. The Mozzarella and Soy is more bland."*

1 cup (240 ml) cooked ground goat
½ cup (120 ml) chopped onion
1 cup (240 ml) coarsely chopped tomatoes
2 cups (480 ml) chopped zucchini or 2 cups chopped
   broccoli
1½ cups (360 ml) grated cheese
½ cup (120 ml) flour
½ teaspoon (2.5 ml) baking powder
½ teaspoon (2.5 ml) salt
¼ teaspoon (1.25 ml) pepper
2 eggs
1 cup (240 ml) goat milk

Sprinkle the vegetable, meat, and cheese on the bottom of a greased 10″ (25 cm) pie plate.

Mix the eggs, flour and seasonings in a blender for 10 to 15 seconds.

Pour the liquid over the vegetable.

Bake for 40 minutes at 400°F/200°C/Gas 6 until golden brown.

## Curry of Goat
*4 servings*

*While not a traditional curry, this easy-to-do dish has all the flavor and aroma of the real thing. And, it only uses one pan.*

1 lb (450 g) of ground goat, browned
3 apples, sliced
2 tablespoons (30 ml) butter
1 onion, thinly sliced
1 clove garlic, peeled and shopped
3 tablespoons (45 ml) flour
1 tablespoon (15 ml) curry powder
1 tablespoon (15 ml) lemon juice
2 cups (480 ml) vegetable broth
⅓ cup (80 ml) raisins
4 cloves

In a large frying pan, brown the goat meat in butter, and set aside. Sauté the apples, onion and garlic in the same butter. Blend in the curry powder and flour to the apple mixture. Stir in gradually the vegetable broth and lemon juice. Add the raisins and cloves.

Cover and simmer for 20 minutes.

Add the browned goat meat and simmer for an additional 10 minutes.

Serve over rice and have a side dish of chutney.

The person who finds the first clove gets a wish — it usually comes true!

# Pat's Goat-Loaf Muffins

6 servings

*A simple and fast way to cook and serve "diner-style" meat loaf.*

1 teaspoon (5 ml) olive oil
1 cup (240 ml) sweet onion, chopped very fine
½ cup (120 ml) carrot, chopped fine
1 teaspoon (5 ml) oregano
2 cloves of garlic, minced
1 cup (240 ml) tomato ketchup, divided
1½ lb (680 g) ground goat
1 cup (240 ml) (about 20) saltine crackers, crushed
  very fine
2 tablespoons (30 ml) prepared yellow mustard
1 teaspoon (5 ml) Worcestershire sauce
¼ teaspoon (1.25 ml) black pepper
2 large eggs

Preheat the oven to 350°F/180°C/Gas 4
Grease 12 muffin cups (you can use cooking spray).
Heat the olive oil in a large skillet. Add the vegetables and herbs and spices. Sauté for about 2 minutes and then allow to cool.
In a large bowl, combine the vegetable mixture with half the ketchup and the remaining ingredients. Mix well.
Spoon the mixture into the muffin cups and top each wit 2 teaspoons of the remaining ketchup.
Bake at 350°F/180°C/Gas 4 for 25 minutes, or until the tops are browned.
Let them stand for 5 minutes before removing.

# Goat Quesadillas
*4 servings*

*Perfect Patio Party food! This cheese-filled delight will be a hit with your guests.*

> 1 cup (240 ml) cooked ground goat meat
> 1 tablespoon (15 ml) olive oil
> 1 medium red onion, peeled and slivered
> Eight 7½" (190 mm) flour tortillas
> 4 oz (120 ml) white goat cheese, grated
> 4 oz (120 g) Monterey jack cheese, grated
> 4 large mushrooms, washed and thinly sliced
> 2 scallions, chopped fine
> 1 tablespoon (15 ml) chopped fresh mint or parsley

Place the oil in a non stick skillet over low heat. Add the onion and stir and cook for 10 minutes until wilted. Set aside.

Cover the 4 tortillas with 1 tablespoon (45 ml) each goat cheese and jack cheese, covering the tortillas evenly.

Evenly layer the cooked goat meat, onions, mushrooms, scallions, mint and remaining cheese. Press these down.

Heat a large, dry skillet over medium heat until very hot. Using a spatula, place a quesadilla in the skillet, pressing down once while it cooks, until the cheese melts and the tortilla browns slightly, Turn and lightly brown the other side.

Remove to a 250°F/130°C/Gas ½ oven.

Repeat with the remaining quesadillas,

Cut the quesadillas into quarters, and serve with salsa and guacamole.

## Greek Goat Loaf

*4 servings*

*We are willing to bet that you have all the ingredients in your pantry to create this tasty goat meat loaf that will impart a Grecian flavor.*

Preheat the oven to 350°F/180°C/Gas 4.

1 slice of whole-wheat bread
½ white onion, peeled and sliced
1 garlic clove, crushed
1 egg, slightly beaten
1 teaspoon (5 ml) lemon zest
2 tablespoons (30 ml) lemon juice
1 lb (450 g) ground goat
1 teaspoon (5 ml) dill weed
½ teaspoon (2.5 ml) oregano
¼ teaspoon (1.25 ml) salt
¼ teaspoon (1.25 ml) pepper

Tear the bread into pieces and crumble into crumbs.

In a large bowl, combine the onions, garlic, egg, lemon zest and juice. and crumbs. Mix well. Add the goat meat and herbs and spices, blend again.

Pack into a loaf pan and bake for 50–60 minutes or until the juices run clear and the loaf is slightly browned.

## *Mediterranean Goat Burgers*  4 servings

*You won't find these at the Golden Arches. The surprising addition of spinach, paired with feta cheese and Kalamata olives brings the flavor of the blue Mediterranean right to your grill!*

1 lb (450 g) ground goat
⅛ cup (30 ml) feta cheese
¼ cup (60 ml) chopped spinach or frozen spinich
  (squeeze out excess water)
¼ cup (60 ml) chopped and pitted Kalamata olives
⅛ teaspoon (30 ml) ground black pepper

Mix all the ingredients well and form into four patties. Broil to preferred doneness. But do not overcook—goat is best served medium to medium rare.

# *Porcupine Meatballs*

24–48 *meatballs*

*Patricia says: "My mother, Sharron Moore, of Ashland Oregon. made these when I was a kid. I loved them then, and I love them now."*

2 lb (900 g) ground goat meat
½ cup (120 ml) raw white rice
2 tablespoons (30 ml) onion, minced
2 teaspoons (10 ml) salt
½ teaspoon (2.5 ml) black pepper
1 cup (240 ml) tomato juice
2 tablespoons (30 ml) ketchup
1 tablespoon (15 ml) horseradish
½ teaspoon (2.5 ml) Worcestershire sauce

Mix the ground goat meat, rice, onion, salt and pepper, and shape into ½" (1.25 cm) or 1" (2.5 cm) meatballs and place them in an oven-proof casserole dish.

Mix the tomato juice with the rest of the ingredients. Pour over the meatballs and bake at 350°F/180°C/Gas 4, covered, for 45 minutes.

## Mexican Goat
## & Vegetable Pie

*12 servings*

*¡Olé! A wonderful main course or as an appetizer.*

1 lb (450 g) ground goat
1 cup (240 ml) onion, peeled and chopped fine
3 garlic cloves, minced and divided
½ cup (120 ml) green onions, sliced
½ cup (120 ml) green bell pepper, seeded and chopped
1½ cup (360 ml) frozen or fresh whole kernel corn
½ cup (120 ml) picante sauce
2 tablespoons (30 ml) cilantro, minced
2 tablespoons (30 ml) lime juice
Two 16 oz (475 ml) cans pinto beans, drained
2 medium tomatoes, chopped
½ cup (120 ml) all-purpose flour
½ cup (120 ml) yellow cornmeal
½ teaspoon (2.5 ml) chili powder
1 cup (240 ml) skim milk
4 eggs, lightly beaten
1 cup (240 ml) shredded cheddar cheese
¼ cup (60 ml) sour cream
Cooking spray
Sour cream to garnish

Coat a non-stick skillet with the cooking spry and heat over medium-high. Add the onions and sauté until tender. Add the goat meat and 1 minced garlic clove. Cook until browned and crumbled, Remove from the pan.

Wipe the skillet with a paper towel and coat again. Add the green onions, bell pepper and the remaining garlic. Sauté until tender. Stir in the corn, picante sauce, cilantro, lime juice, pinto beans and tomatoes, then add the goat, onion and garlic mixture to this. Cook until heated through. Remove from the heat.

Combine the flour, cornmeal and chili powder in a medium bowl. Gradually add the milk and eggs, stirring until well-blended.

Into two 9″ (230 mm) pie plates that have been coated with cooking oil divide the flour and cornmeal mixture.

Bake at 475°F/240°C/Gas 9 for 10 minutes until puffed and golden.

Let cool slightly before spooning half the goat mixture into each pie shell then sprinkle with the cheese.

Bake at 475°F/240°C/Gas 9 for 1 minute or until the cheese melts.

Cut each pie into 6 pieces.

Garnish with sour cream.

## Sesame Goat Meatballs   24 large meatballs

*The Sheikh of Araby would love these meatballs, coated in sesame with a hint of mint. Serve this with a bowl of minted yoghurt sauce. Couscous would be an ideal starch, or pita bread. If you make the meatballs quite small (walnut size) they are perfect as part of a buffet table. Provide toothpicks and a camel.*

1 small onion, peeled and chopped fine
1 large garlic clove, peeled and chopped fine
1½ tablespoons (7.5 ml) olive oil
½ teaspoon (2.5 ml) dried mint leaves
½ teaspoon (2.5 ml) sea salt
½ teaspoon (2.5 ml) cinnamon
1 lb (450 g) ground goat meat
1 cup (240 ml) bread crumbs
1 large egg, beaten
2 tablespoons (30 ml) currants
½ cup (120 ml) sesame seeds, toasted lightly
2 cups (480 ml) plain yoghurt
¼ cup (60 ml) fresh mint leaves, washed and chopped fine
½ teaspoon (2.5 ml) sea salt to taste

In a large sauté pan, heat the olive oil. Add the onion and garlic and sauté until golden. Remove from the pan into a large bowl.

Into the bowl, put in the dried mint, salt,cinnamon, goat meat, bread crumbs, the beaten egg and the currants. Mix well with your hands.

Using your hands, which are wet, form this mixture into meatballs, the size of a golf ball. Roll the meatballs in the sesame to coat.

Place the meatballs on a baking sheet and bake at 425°F/215°C/Gas 7 for 10 minutes.

To make the minted yoghurt, simply mix the fresh mint leaves into the yoghurt, add a bit of salt to taste. Allow this to stand for at least ½ hour for the flavor to develop.

# Sunday Brunch Chevon

8 servings

*A perfect brunch dish, easily prepared and low in fat.*

1 tablespoon (15 ml) olive oil
¼ lb fresh mushrooms, stemmed and sliced
1 yellow onion, chopped
¾ lb ground goat meat
8 eggs
1 cup (240 ml) of cream of mushroom soup, (low-fat and sodium) undiluted
1 cup (240 ml) of non-fat milk
3 cups (720) bread cubes
3 tablespoons (45 ml) fresh basil, chopped coarsely
½ cup (120 ml) Parmesan cheese
Fresh chopped parsley

Heat the olive oil in a sauté pan and add the onions and mushrooms. Sauté lightly. Add the goat. Stir until browned. Cool.

In a medium bowl, mix the eggs, mushroom soup and milk together, beating with a fork. Stir in the basil and the bread cubes.

Add the onions, mushroom and goat meat mix and blend together well.

Pour into a 8" x 11" x 2" (20 x 28 x 5 cm) baking dish and let stand in the refrigerator for one hour or until ready to cook.

Bake at 350°F/180°C/Gas 4 for 30 minutes. Let stand for 10 minutes before cutting into squares.

Sprinkle with the Parmesan cheese and parsley before serving.

# Swedish Meatballs *24 large or 48 small meatballs*

*Here is a tasty morsel with cocktails or a main dish, depending on how large you form the meatballs.*

1 lb. (450 g) ground goat meat
½ cup (120 ml) dry bread crumbs
⅓ cup (80 ml) onion minced
¼ cup (60 ml) goats milk
1 medium egg
1 tablespoon (15 ml) parsley
1 teaspoon (5 ml) salt
½ teaspoon (2.5 ml) black pepper
½ teaspoon (2.5 ml) Worcestershire sauce
¼ cup (60 ml) shortening

Mix ground goat meat, crumbs, onion, milk, egg, and next 4 seasonings until well mixed. Gently shape into ½" (1.25 cm) or 1" (2.5 cm) meatballs.

Melt the shortening in a large skillet and brown the meatballs on all sides. Remove meatballs from skillet and drain on paper towels.

Provide toothpicks and serve with dips (sour cream and dill would be good!) as an appetizer or serve with chopped parsley and egg noodles.

## Sweet Potato Goatherd's Pie   8 servings

*Smokey spicy chipotle chilies and adobo sauce cut the*
*sweetness of the sweet potato topping and they add a kick!*

For the topping:
   One 6 oz (180 ml) can chipotle chilies in adobo
      sauce
   2½ lb (1.13 kg) peeled sweet potatoes, cut into 1"
      (2.5 cm) pieces
   1 cup (240 ml) milk
   1 teaspoon (5 ml) salt
   ¼ teaspoon (1.25 ml) pepper

For the filling:
   2 lb (900 g) of ground goat meat
   2 cups (480 ml) onion, chopped
   1 cup (240 ml) carrots, chopped
   4 cloves of garlic, minced
   1½ cups (360 ml) green peas
   ½ cup (120 ml) crushed tomatoes
   ¼ cup (60 ml) parsley
   3 tablespoons (45 ml) steak sauce
   2 tablespoons (30 ml) tomato paste
   ½ teaspoon (2.5 ml) black pepper

Preheat the oven to 400°F/200°C/Gas 6.

Place the potatoes in a saucepan and cover with water. Bring to a boil and cook until very tender. Drain.

Coarsely chop one chipotle chili.

Put the drained potatoes and chopped chili and 2 teaspoons (10 ml) of the adobo sauce, milk, salt and pepper in a large bowl. Beat with a mixer until smooth.

Cook the ground goat in a skillet over medium-high heat until browned. Stirring to crumble the meat.

Add the onion, carrot and garlic. Sauté for 8–10 minutes or until the vegetables are tender. Return the goat meat to the pan, stir in the peas and the remaining ingredients. Cook for 2 minutes.

Spoon the meat mixture into a 10″ (250 mm) pie plate and top with the sweet potato mixture.

Bake at 400°F/200°C/Gas 6 for 30 minutes or until the top is browned.

# Three-layer Goat Casserole   6 servings

*This is simple, fast and quite good. You can make this ahead of time and keep it in the refrigerator for up to 24 hours.*

2 lbs (900 g) ground goat
2 cloves of garlic, minced
1 sweet onion, chopped fine
Two 15 oz (440 ml) cans tomato sauce
1 tablespoon (15 ml) dried basil
One 8–10 oz (225–285 g) package spinach fettucini
  noodles
1 cup (240 ml) shredded sharp cheddar cheese
One 8 oz (240 ml) package cream cheese
1 cup (240 ml) sour cream
1 cup (240 ml) milk

Brown the goat meat in a skillet until browned and crumbled.

Mix in the garlic, onion, tomato sauce and basil. Cover and simmer for 30 minutes.

Cook the fettucini in boiling water, uncovered, for 8 minutes or until tender. Drain.

In a 4 quart (4 liter) casserole dish, spoon the meat mixture in first, then top with the noodles. Sprinkle the cheese on the top evenly.

Blend the cream cheese, sour cream and milk until smooth. Pour over the noodles and meat.

Bake at 350°F/180°C/Gas 4 for 45 minutes.

# *Patty's Wonderful Meatballs* 6 servings

*Served over fettucini with your favorite red or white sauce, this makes a great meal. These flavorful meatballs can also be made much smaller for an appetizer.*

1 lb (450 g) ground goat
1 egg, lightly beaten
¾ teaspoon (3.75 ml) nutmeg
Half a lemon, zested
¼ cup (60 ml) bread crumbs
½ teaspoon (2.5 ml) pepper
½ teaspoon (2.5 ml) salt

Mix all of the above in a medium-sized bowl.
Wet your hands and make into golf-ball sized meatballs.
Put them on a baking sheet.
Bake at 350°F/180°C/Gas 4 until done, about 15 minutes.

**Yogurt Dipping Dressing** (for an appetizer):

¼ cup (60 ml) sour cream
1 teaspoon (5 ml) lemon juice
½ cup (120 ml) chopped mint, fresh or dried
⅛ teaspoon (0.6 ml) paprika
1½ cups (360 ml) yoghurt
¼ teaspoon (1.25 ml) pepper

Mix in a bowl. Refrigerate.
Provide toothpicks for the meatballs and serve them hot.

*Don't approach a goat from the front, a horse from the back, or a fool from any side.*
— Yiddish Proverb

# On the Side

*Ideas are easy. It's the execution of ideas that really separates the sheep from the goats.*

—Sue Grafton

# Ginger & Red Onion Chutney

240 ml (4 cups)

*This chutney is unlike any chutney you have tasted before.*
*It is wonderful with all the goat stews on the side, or,*
*spoon it over soft goat cheese and pass the crackers!*

1 medium red onion, peeled and chopped
2 tablespoons (30 ml) butter
2 tablespoons (30 ml) vegetable oil
½ cup (120 ml) red wine vinegar
½ cup (120 ml) Balsamic vinegar
½ cup (120 ml) apple cider vinegar
1 cup (240 ml) sugar
⅓ cup (80 ml) chopped, candied ginger

Caramelize the onion by heating the butter and oil in a heavy skillet. Add the onions and a small amount of sugar and slowly cook over medium heat about 30–40 minutes, stirring often, until the onion is caramel coloured.

Add the vinegar's, remaining sugar and ginger. Continue to cook down to a syrup consistency.

## Gremolata
*2 servings*

*Gremolata (or gremolada) is a chopped herb condiment. Although it is a common accompaniment to veal, the citrus element in gremolata makes it an appropriate addition to goat dishes. Steven Hazell from Bend, Oregon, likes to use this with his goat dishes.*

    2 tablespoons (30 ml) fresh, flat-leafed parsley
    leaves (wash and dry before chopping
    1 teaspoon (5 ml) minced garlic (about 1 large
    clove)
    1 teaspoon (5 ml) freshly grated lemon zest
    1 teaspoon (5 ml) grated lime zest
    1 teaspoon (5 ml) frshely grated orange zest
    1 teaspoon (5 ml) chopped fresh rosemary
    Black pepper to taste
    Salt to taste

In a small bowl, stir together all the ingredients. Season with pepper and salt to taste

## Hummus

Many cuisine-related sources carry forward a folklore which describes hummus as one of the oldest known prepared foods. it has a a long history in the Middle East which stretches back to antiquity, but its historical origins are unknown. One of the earliest verifiable descriptions of hummus comes from 18th-century Damascus and the same source claims it was unknown elsewhere. Hummus is popular today because of its low fat and cholesterol. The flavors remain the same as 1,000 years ago

Two 15 oz (440 ml) cans chickpeas, drained
⅓ cup (80 ml) sesame tahini
Juice of 1 lemon (about ¼ cup (60 ml))
⅓ cup (80 ml) water
2 cloves garlic, peeled and thinly sliced
½ teaspoon (2.5 ml) cumin
1 teaspoon (5 ml) salt
1 tablespoon (15 ml) olive oil

Combine the chickpeas, tahini, lemon juice, water, garlic, cumin, and salt in a food processor and pulse until chunky smooth, about 10 to 15 seconds.

Serve with fresh pita bread.

## Moroccan Chickpea Ragout   *4 servings*

*If you serve this over couscous, you have a traditional meal, full of Moroccan flavors!*

2 tablespoons (30 ml) extra-virgin olive oil
1 red onion, diced
2 tablespoons (30 ml) minced garlic
1 teaspoon (5 ml) cumin
Two 15 oz (440 mml) cans chickpeas drained and
  rinsed
One 14 oz (415 ml) can diced tomatoes
½ teaspoon (2.5 ml) dried thyme
2 teaspoons (10 ml) honey
2 teaspoons (10 ml) fresh lemon juice
1¾ cups (420 ml) chicken or vegetable broth
Salt and pepper to taste
½ cup (120 ml) flat-leaf parsley, chopped

Heat the oil in a heavy saucepan over medium-low heat.

Add the onion and garlic. Cook for 5 minutes until wilted and transparent. Sprinkle with the cumin and stir.

Stir in the chickpeas, tomatoes, thyme, honey, lemon juice and broth.

Bring to a boil, reduce the heat to low. Season with salt and pepper and simmer for 4 minutes.

Stir in the parsley.

# Raisin & Almond Couscous    4 servings

*For centuries, couscous has been a staple in the Mediterranean countries. An abundance of almonds as well as golden raisins added to the nutty flavour of the couscous is a delight to the palette and a good side dish to goat meat, especially grilled goat.*

1½ cups (360 ml) water
⅓ cup (80 ml) golden raisins
1 teaspoon (5 ml) salt
¾ cup (180 ml) couscous
¼ teaspoon (1.25 ml) ground cumin
¼ teaspoon (1.25 ml) ground coriander
¼ teaspoon (1.25 ml) ground black pepper
¼ cup (60 ml) sliced almonds
¼ cup (60 ml) chopped flat leaf parsley

In a medium saucepan, combine the water, raisins and ½ teaspoon (2.5 ml) of the salt. Bring to a boil, then add the couscous. Remove the pan from the heat, cover and let stand for 5 minutes. Fluff with a fork, cover again and set aside.

In a small bowl, combine the remaining salt, cumin, coriander and pepper.

In a small skillet, stir and toast the almonds over medium heat for about three minutes or until lightly browned.

Add the spices, toasted almonds and parley to the couscous mixture and stir to combine.

## White Bean & Rosemary Ragout

*4 servings*

A perfect side dish for leg of goat, goat burgers, Mediterranean goat... a perfect side dish.

1¾ cups (420 ml) canned cannellini beans, drained,
  liquid reserved
1 tablespoon (15 ml) rosemary
1 teaspoon (5 ml) lemon zest
Salt and freshly ground pepper to taste

In a medium saucepan, combine the cannellini beans, ½ cup (120 ml) of their reserved liquid, the rosemary and lemon zest

Bring this to a simmer over medium heat, stirring constantly, Reduce the heat to low, and continue to simmer the ragout for 10 minutes, stirring occasionally. If the ragout becomes too thick, add 2 to 3 tablespoons (30–45 ml) of the reserved liquid to restore consistency, which should be like cooked oatmeal,

# Scalloped Potatoes à la Zap    4 servings

*Need something in a hurry? Your microwave awaits!*

5 medium potatoes, sliced
1½ cups (360 ml) goat milk, scalded
3 tablespoons (45 ml) flour
1 teaspoon (5 ml) salt
4 slices goat cheese
2 tablespoons (30 ml) butter

Arrange half of the potatoes in a medium, microwave-proof greased casserole

Mix the flour and salt, then sprinkle half over the potatoes. Put two slices of the cheese over the potatoes.

Repeat by adding the remaining potatoes, flour and salt combination and cheese.

Slice the butter on the top and then pour the scalded milk over it all.

Microwave on High, uncovered, for 15–20 minutes or until the potatoes are tender.

If you don't have a microwave that has a rotating dish, turn the casserole once during cooking.

# Stuffed Peppers

*6 servings*

Choose your pepper colour to match your recipe. Mexican? Try red peppers. Mideast? Yellow or orange would look well. Plain everyday recipes would want green peppers. Vary your spices if you want.

1 cup (240 ml) dry orzo
2 tablespoons (30 ml) olive oil
1 sweet onion, peeled and chopped
2 celery stalks, peeled and chopped
3 garlic cloves, peeled and chopped
2 cups (480 ml) feta or goat cheese, crumbled
¼ teaspoon (1.25 ml) black pepper
½ teaspoon (2.5 ml) salt
¼ cup (1.25 ml) mint leaves, chopped (fresh or dried)
6 peppers, red, orange green or yellow or mixed
1½ cups (360 ml) tomato juice

Cut the tops off the peppers and remove the seeds and white membrane. Leave enough room to fill. Slice a small part off the bottom so they sit upright.

Cook the orzo and drain.

In a skillet, heat the olive oil and sauté the onion, celery and garlic until they are transparent. Stir in the cooked orzo, mint, salt , pepper and cheese.

Fill the pepper cups with the orzo mixture and stand them upright in a pan large enough to hold all of them.

Pour the juice over them and bring them to a boil. Reduce the heat and simmer, covered, for 20 minutes. The peppers should be tender but not falling apart.

# Tomato Confit

*8 servings*

*The word confit comes from the French verb "confire", meaning 'to preserve', which in turn comes from the Latin word "conficere" meaning 'to do, to produce, to make, to prepare'. The French verb was first applied in medieval times to fruits cooked and preserved in sugar. This sweet yet spicy tomato mixture will compliment all your goat dishes.*

> 3 cups (about 1 lb) (720 ml (about 450 g)) ripe plum tomatoes, chopped
> 1½ cups (about ½ pound) (360 ml (about 225 g)) grape tomatoes, cut in half
> ½ cup (120 ml) sugar
> 1 teaspoon (5 ml) cinnamon
> ½ teaspoon (2.5 ml) red pepper flakes

In a large saucepan combine all the ingredients.

Bring to a boil, stirring to prevent burning

Reduce the heat to medium and cook over medium-low for about 35 minutes. You want this to thicken. Stir often.

Remove from the heat.

Place in a bowl.

This will keep in your refrigerator for up to three days, covered.

## Zorba's Potatoes
*4 servings*

*This good potato dish is good with all the chops and shanks!*

10–12 red potatoes
3 tablespoons (45 ml) olive oil
½ cup (120 ml) chopped green onions (tops and all)
2 tablespoons (30 ml) oregano
2 tablespoons (30 ml) lemon juice
2 teaspoons (10 ml) minced garlic
1 teaspoon (5 ml) paprika
1 teaspoon (5 ml) black pepper
1 teaspoon (5 ml) salt
½ cup (120 ml) feta goat cheese, crumbled

Boil the potatoes until just soft. Drain. Cool and slice into ½" (2.5 cm) pieces.

In a skillet, heat the olive oil and sauté the potatoes until browned on all sides.

Add the remaining ingredients except the feta cheese.

Stir and toss well. Cover the skillet and cook for 5 minutes longer on medium heat.

Top with the feta goat cheese.

# *Desserts*

# Getting Your Goat

Put silk on a goat and it is still a goat.
—Irish saying

# Goat Cheese Custards

*Creamy and rich, these are the perfect end to a delicious dinner. Fresh, sugared and quartered strawberries on top and—violà!*

> 5 oz (140 g) fresh goat cheese, at room temperature
> ¼ cup (60 ml) sugar
> ½ cup (120 ml) milk, cream, or half-and-half
> 2 large egg yolks
> ⅛ teaspoon (0.6 ml) vanilla extract

Preheat the oven to 350°F/180°C/Gas 4. Place four custard cups or ramekins in a deep baking dish or pan.

Blend together the goat cheese, sugar, milk (or cream), egg yolks, and vanilla for 30 seconds until very smooth.

Divide the mixture into the custard cups; each should be a bit more than half full.

Add warm tap water to the baking pan, to make a water bath for baking the custards. The water should reach to about halfway up the side of each custard cup.

Cover the pan with foil and bake for 15–20 minutes.

When done, remove the custards from the water bath and cool completely.

**Storage and serving**: Custards are best served at room temperature. They can be chilled up to two days in the refrigerator, covered with plastic wrap, then brought to room temperature prior to serving.

# *You Scream for Ice Cream*    8 servings

*Here is a wonderful and healthy ice cream from Susan Conner of Sisters, Oregon. Susan's goats are a Boer/dairy cross and she says that 90% of her cooking is done with goat meat and milk.*

1½ cups (360 ml) white sugar
¼ cup (60 ml) corn starch
¼ teaspoon (1.25 ml) salt
8 cups (1.9 litres) fresh goat milk
3 eggs, beaten
1 teaspoon (5 ml) unflavored gelatine
1½ tablespoons (22.5 ml) vanilla

Mix the sugar, cornstarch and salt in the top of a double boiler.

Add 4 cups (950 ml) of milk gradually.

Cook over hot water about 15 minutes or until thickened.

Beat the eggs and add the cornstarch. Add the egg mixture into the milk.

Continue cooking about 10 minutes until it starts to thicken.

Stir the gelatine into 1 cup (240 ml) of milk and stir in.

Chill mixture thoroughly.

Then add the remaining 3 cups (720 ml) of milk and the vanilla and out into an ice cream maker and freeze.

# An Irish Ice Cream Secret

*Our friend Jon from County Down relates the following anecdote from his friend Dominic about the right milk to use for making goat-milk ice cream.*

"If your goats are not fed on anything but grass, you can make a tasty ice cream all right—but you'll be missing out on a dreamy treat!

"If your goats have been fed purely on grass—no silage, no hay—the ice cream you can make from them will be *unbelievably* creamy.

"You'll have Ben & Jerry wanting to send the Mafia round to your door out of jealousy. But never mind about them— the mother who is worried about dairy products and what to give her children will be happy and contented indeed to offer them such rich, creamy, and healthy ice cream!"

> It's difficult to choose between two blind goats.
>
> —*Irish proverb*

# Carrot Cake with
# Goat Cheese Frosting
*8 servings*

*A perfect combination of a rich, dark cake with a goat cheese frosting to top it off.*

For the cake:
- 2 cups (480 ml) flour
- 1½ cups (360 ml) granulated sugar
- 2¼ teaspoons (11.25 ml) baking soda
- 1½ teaspoons (7.5 ml) baking powder
- 1½ teaspoons (7.5 ml) cinnamon
- ¼ teaspoon (1.25 ml) ground cloves
- ¼ teaspoon ground (1.25 ml) nutmeg
- ⅛ teaspoon (0.6 ml) freshly ground black pepper
- ¼ teaspoon (1.25 ml) salt
- 1 cup (240 ml) vegetable oil
- 4 large eggs lightly beaten
- 3 cups (720 ml) packed coarsely grated carrots (about 6 medium carrots)
- 1 cup (240 ml) coarsely chopped walnuts, plus more for garnish

For the frosting:
- 10 oz (280 g) fresh, mild chèvre (goat cheese), at room temperature
- 8 oz (225 ml) cream cheese, at room temperature
- 2 tablespoons (30 ml) unsalted butter, at room temperature
- 1 teaspoon (5 ml) vanilla extract
- 2 cups (480 ml) powdered sugar

Preheat oven to 350°F/180°C/Gas 4. Grease three 9″ (23 cm) round cake pans and set aside.

In a large bowl, combine flour, granulated sugar, baking soda, baking powder, spices, pepper, and salt. Whisk to combine, then stir in oil and eggs. Stir in the carrots and walnuts.

Divide the batter among the pans. Bake until the cakes pull away from pan sides and a cake tester (a toothpick works well) inserted in each center comes out clean, about 25 minutes.

Transfer the cakes to cooling racks. Cool for 10 minutes. Turn out onto racks and let cool completely.

Beat the goat cheese, cream cheese, butter, and vanilla until smooth and fluffy, about 3 minutes. Gradually add powdered sugar and mix until combined.

Once cakes are cool, arrange first layer on a large plate or platter. Spread some frosting over it, then top with second layer. Frost second layer and top with the third. Generously frost top and sides of cake with remaining frosting.

Chill the cake at least 1 hour to allow the frosting to set up.

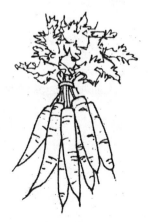

# *Fromage Blanc Cheesecake*    10 *servings*

*Born in Yorkshire, England, Dee Harley's life is surrounded by good friends, good family—and really good food. Realizing her dream of blending family, local farming and gourmet food, Dee started Harley Farms, located in Pescadero California fourteen years ago with just six goats. She rebuilt a 1910 cow dairy farm that now houses the cheese making room and milking parlor - and scattered across her 9 acre (3.6 ha) farm roam 220 American Alpine goats who produce over 500 kids each Spring (definitely the time to visit!). Tradition and family are at the root of Harley Farms. And you can taste it in the cheese. To obtain the cheese, see page 146 below to contact Harley Farms.*

Crust:
   ¾ cup (180 ml) graham cracker crumbs
   ¾ cup (180 ml) chopped white chocolate
   ¾ cup (180 ml) toasted almond brittle
   ¼ cup (60 ml) melted butter

Filling:
   ½ (120 ml) cup sugar, plus another ½ cup (120 ml)
   1 lb (450 g) fromage blanc
   3 sheets gelatin, softened in cool water
   6 yolks
   1½ cups (360 ml) heavy cream whipped to stiff
      peaks

Combine first four ingredients until well coated with butter. Press into bottom of 4″ (100 mm) ring molds. Chill.

Combine ½ cup (120 ml) sugar and fromage blanc in large bowl, whisk over a hot water bath until sugar has dissolved. Squeeze all water out of gelatin sheets and add to warm fromage mixture, stir until gelatin has dissolved. Cool slightly over a water bath until slightly thickened. Whip yolks in mixer with second ½ cup (120 ml) of sugar until thick and pale, fold into fromage mixture. Carefully fold in whipped cream. Fill 4″ (100 mm) ring molds, smooth tops and chill until set.

Serve with fresh strawberries on the top. Or, make a strawberry mint salsa by combining strawberries, cut up, chopped fresh mint and sugar to taste.

*If you're short of trouble, get a goat!*

*—Anonymous*

# Miscellaneous

*It don't take a genius to spot a goat in a flock of sheep.*

—Cowboy saying

# Cooking with a slow-cooker

*A slow cooker can be your best friend. There are so many benefits to using a slow-cooker or crock pot.*

- Easy cleanup—usually just one pot.
- Environmentally friendly because it uses less energy than a cook top or oven.
- You can set it up and walk away. No need to adjust or stir.
- Goat meat naturally pairs up with this type of slow, moist cooking.

Read the directions for your slow cooker before you use it. Become familiar with the temperature settings and times.

When using a slow cooker, make sure the pieces of goat meat are a uniform size for even cooking. Browning (braising) the meat before putting it in the slow cooker adds more flavour and appearance to the dish.

Dried beans may take longer to cook. Soaking them overnight in water helps to ensure the beans are tender. If you use canned beans, rinse them and add them during the last hour of cooking. Vegetables like onions and carrots take longer to cook and do best at the bottom of the cooker with the meat placed onto I personally like to lightly sauté the onions, celery, and carrots for about 3 minutes, then place them into the pot.

Keep the lid on! Removing the lid during cooking releases a lot of heat. Each time you "peek" you have to add 20–30 minutes of cooking time. Safety tips:

- Keep meats refrigerated until you use them.
- When possible, cook all meats on High for the first hour.
- Don't cook meat that is still frozen.
- If the power goes out and you are not at home, throw the food away.

# *Lavender Soap*   *Ten 3" x 2" (76 x 50 mm) soaps*

*Breeze Edmonds' Alpine milk goat farm on the Olympic Peninsula has an abundance of lavender. She likes to combine that bounty in this recipe for soap. She says, "You mix fats and an alkali (lye) to make any soap, which is caustic. You must wear goggles (or glasses) when you make soap. Wear rubber gloves and long sleeves too. The finished soap is harmless and so good for your skin! It is a bit time consuming, but the end result makes wonderful gifts for your friends and, of course, for you."*

2 stainless steel cooking pots
1 plastic or glass container
Rubber spatula
Cooking thermometer, 90–200°F (30–100°C) range
Plastic storage tub that holds at least 2 cups (480 ml). Grease it lightly with petroleum jelly for easy removal of the soap.
Hand-held stick blender (optional)
Wax or parchment paper

11 ounces (320 g) coconut oil
12 ounces (330 g) palm oil
15.5 ounces (440 g) olive oil
4 ounces (110 g) almond oil
6 ounces (175 g) Red Devil lye
15.5 ounces (440 g) whole goat's milk
2⅓ (35 ml) tablespoons lavender essential oil
1 tablespoon (15 ml) almond oil

First, measure the oils (but not the lavender or almond oil) and combine them in one of the stainless steel pans. Heat them slowly, stirring, until everything melts, then cool to about 110°F/43°C.

Measure the lye into the plastic or glass container. (Did you remember the gloves and goggles or glasses?)

Now measure the goat milk and pour it into the other stainless steel pan. and bring the milk almost up to a boil.

*Slowly* pour the lye into the milk, stirring constantly with the spatula. Keep the milk temperature below 150°F/65°C. When all the lye is added, let the mixture cool until it is 110°F/43°C.

Then add the lye/milk mixture to the oils, stirring. Turn the heat up under the pan to medium-high. Stir the soap mixture for about 45 minutes until it begins to gel. Stop stirring when a thin stream of soap drizzled from the spoon on top of the soap mixture stays on top.

*A trick to speed things is to use a hand blender. Blend the soap for 30 seconds, let it rest for a minute and repeat until the drizzle lays on the top of the mixture.*

Now you can add the lavender oil and almond oil, stirring them in gently.

Pour the soap mix into the plastic tub (did you remember to grease it first?). Cover with a damp towel and let the soap sit and solidify for 24 hours.

Turn the tub upside-down to release the soap.

Cut the soap into bars (the size is your choice). Put the new bars aside on waxed or parchment paper to cure for 4 weeks. A well-ventilated place is best. Keep them covered.

# About Raw Dogfood

At Sand Lily Farm, our livestock guardian dogs thrive on a raw meat diet. Encouraged by Hillrest Border Collie breeder Brittney MacNeill, our dogs are fed a combination of goat meat and kibble. Brittney has found that most dogs experience "large improvements" in their health immediately after changing to a raw diet or a combination of both raw and commercial dog kibble.

The goal of our ranch is making sure our dogs live a balanced life of good health. The basic principals with feeding a raw/combination diet are to give our dogs that wild food such as other canine species such as wolves eat. Raw provides increased resistance to degenerative diseases, such as arthritis, naturally clean teeth which prevents gum disease, and gives them more time to stimulate the positive digestive acids. Raw also provides better weight control; longer life spans and more appropriate growth rates .

# Luscious Goat Dinner for Dogs

2 cups (480 ml) goat meat (chopped finely or ground)
1 cup (240 ml) brown or white rice, cooked
½ large carrot, grated
½ cup (120 ml) plain, 2% yoghurt
1 clove garlic, peeled and crushed
1 (5 ml) teaspoon ground flaxseed
2½ (600 ml) cups water

Cook the goat by boiling it in water with the garlic over a low heat, covered, until the goat is tender.

Cook the rice according to package directions, using the water that was used to cook the goat.

Mix the goat mixture, carrot, and flaxseed with the cooked rice.

Mix in yoghurt and serve after cooling.

# Fido's Favorite Dog Treats

This is a popular recipe. Fido is said to be the name of Abraham Lincoln's dog. He was retriever/shepherd mix and was roughly the color of mustard. Fido is also a Latin word meaning "I trust".

> 10 lbs (4.5 kg) of ground goat
> One 10.6 oz (300 g) box high fiber, high
>     vitamin/mineral content cereal
> One 18 oz (510 g) box oatmeal
> One 12 oz (340 g) wheat germ
> 1¼ cup (300 ml) vegetable oil
> 1¼ cup (300 ml) unsulfured molasses
> 10 raw eggs and the shells
> Ten 1.6 oz (45g) sachets of unflavored gelatin
> A pinch of salt

Mix all the ingredients together, much as you would mix a meatloaf.

Divide into ten 1-quart (1 liter) freezer bags and freeze. Thaw as needed and feed raw!

# "Good Dog!" Dog Treats

*Nothing says love to your four-footed best friend than home-made treats do. These are nutritious, easy to make, and your furry friend will thank you for them. Good dog!*

1 lb (450 g) raw goat liver
2 cloves garlic
1 egg
½ cup (120 ml) molasses
2 cups (480 ml) organic flour

In a blender or food processor, puree the liver, garlic, egg and molasses.

Transfer to a bowl. Add the flour, a little at a time, until it is well-mixed.

Pour onto a greased 9" x 13" cookie sheet. Spread it evenly.

Bake at 350°F/180°C/Gas 4 for 12–15 minutes. Do not overbake.

When it is cool, cut into small cubes or strips.

This can be frozen, or keep in an air-tight jar.

# About Sand Lily Farm

In 1988, Patricia A. Moore and her partner Cheryl Powers purchased 80 acres just outside of the city limits of Bend, Oregon. The property consisted of Ponderosa pine trees, junipers, no road, no water, and no electricity.

Over the next 20 years, the two women have built fences, dug and put in irrigation, dug a large pond, and built a beautiful barn while the snow was flying. Patricia recalls, "Cheryl and I worked on that barn every day, hands-on. All we had was a forklift, a pile of materials, and a goal to get it done." All the outdoor goat structures were built over a period of three years.

It took over six years to build the house, which they designed. They named their growing business *Sand Lily Farm* for the beautiful plants that are native to the area and which are becoming rare. Says Patricia, "As soon as the snow melts, usually in April, suddenly the ground will be covered in little white tufts. They are special and delicate."

Today, Sand Lily Farm has more then twenty acres in organic pasture for their South African Boer meat goats. They boast over 100 does and several bucks. Taking care of the herd are two large Maremma sheep dogs, nine-year-old Gus and two-year-old Max, as well as Geraldine the llama, all of whom see to it that no coyotes or other predators cause trouble, especially when there are tempting kids bouncing around.

The Maremma is a massive gentle giant weighing from 66 to 100 pounds (30 to 45 kg). These dogs, whose large heads are similar to those of bears, with their long thick fur—mostly white to light tan—are ideal for colder weather, yet thrive quite well in the hot summer sun of Central Oregon.

Maremmas are typically born and live amongst the livestock they're expected to protect and often never leave their herd. Puppies often start their duties soon after being weaned.

Because of their large size and long fur, Maremmas do not make very good household pets. They also find it hard to adapt to small quarters and the lack of stimulation which comes from protecting a flock.

In addition to their goat herd, Patricia and Cheryl raise an organic vegetable garden, which, Patricia says, "is a challenge in Central Oregon because our growing season is so short!" A flock of various breeds of chickens give the farm colorful and organic eggs, as well as meat.

Sand Lily Farm is a beautiful and well-managed place, with hawks, owls and bald eagles flying over, deer, coyotes, and the occasional cougar. A peek through the trees of Mount Bachelor just adds to the charm.

"An egg of one hour old, bread of one day, a goat of one month, wine of six months, flesh of a year, fish of ten years, and a wife of twenty years, a friend among a hundred, are the best of all number."
—John Wodroephe, English commentator, 'Spared Hours', 1623

# How to Get Your Goat

# Goat Associations

No matter where you are, you probably aren't very far from a supplier of goat meat, milk, or cheese. On the pages below you will find a variety of organizations around the world which you can contact to find out where you can obtain goat meat, milk, or cheese locally. The links here were current at the time of publication, but of course internet links are sometimes ephemeral. If you find a state or regional link that isn't working, one of the national organizations may be able to help you. We are grateful to Susan Schoenian at **sheepandgoat.com** for many of the links here.

## National Goat Associations in the U.S.

American Dairy Goat Association, adga.org
American Goat Federation, usgoatcouncil.org
American Goat Society, americangoatsociety.com
American Meat Goat Association, meatgoats.com
North American Pack Goat Association, napga.org

## State and Regional Goat Associations in the U.S.

Southeast Arkansas Goat Producers Association,
southeastarkansasgoatproducersassociation.com
Kentucky Goat Producers Association, kentuckygpa.com
Mississippi Goat Association,
mississippigoatassociation.org
North Dakota Goat Association, ndgoats.tripod.com
(*Pennsylvania*) Keystone Goat Producers Association,
keystonegoatproducers.org
(*Tennessee*) Southern Regional Goat Association,
thesrga.com
(*Texas*) Freestone County Goat Breeder's Association,
freestonecountygoats.org
(*Texas*) Sam Houston Goat Association,
samhoustongoatassociation.com
South Central Texas Goat Club, sctexgoatclub.org
(*Wisconsin*) Stateline Goat Association,
statelinegoats.com
Southern Highlands Goat Producers Association,
(*Northwest Georgia, Western Alabama, and Southern Tennessee*) sohighgoats.com

## *State Dairy Goat Associations in the U.S.*

Arizona State Dairy Goat Association, asdga.com
Colorado Dairy Goat Association, colodga.org
Florida Dairy Goat Association, fdga.org
Georgia Dairy Goat Breeders Association,
georgiagoat.com
Indiana Dairy Goat Association, idga.net
Iowa Dairy Goat Association, iowadairygoat.org
Maryland Dairy Goat Association, marylanddairygoat.org
Michigan Dairy Goat Society, mdgs.org
Minnesota Dairy Goat Association, minnesotagoats.org
Mississippi Dairy Goat Association, missdairygoat.com
New York State Dairy Goat Breeders Association,
geocities.com/nysdgba
North Carolina Dairy Goat Breeders' Association,
ncdgba.org
Ohio Dairy Goat Association, odga.org
Ohio Valley Dairy Goat Association, kelpies.us/ovdga
Pennsylvania Dairy Goat Association, pdga.biz
Smokey Mountain Dairy Goat Association (*Tennessee*),
angelfire.com/tn2/smdga
Virginia State Dairy Goat Association, vsdga.org
Wisconsin Dairy Goat Association, wdga.org

## Regional Dairy Goat Associations in the U.S.

Southern Arizona Dairy Goat Association, sadga.org
(California) North Valley Dairy Goat Association,
nvdga.org
(California) Redwood Empire Dairy Goat Association,
redga.org
Mid-Ohio Dairy Goat Association, modga.org
North East Ohio Dairy Goat Association, neodga.com
Southeastern Ohio Dairy Goat Association,
buttinheads.com/SEODGA/SEODGA.htm
Northwest Oregon Dairy Goat Association, nwodga.org
Southern Vermont Dairy Goat Association, vtgoats.org
(Wisconsin) Chippewa Valley Dairy Goat Association,
cvdga.org

## Combined Sheep & Goat Associations in the U.S.

Alabama Meat Goat & Sheep Producers,
alfafarmers.org/commodities/meat.phtml
Arkansas Regional Goat, Sheep, & Fiber Producers,
argoatsheepfiber.com
Nebraska Sheep & Goat Producers,
nebraskasheepgoat.org
Western Nebraska Sheep & Goat Association,
wnsga.com
Texas Sheep & Goat Raisers Association, tsgra.com
Vermont Sheep & Goat Association, vermontsheep.org

## State Meat Goat Associations in the U.S.

California Meat Goat Association, camga.org
Florida Meat Goat Association, fmga.org
Georgia Meat Goat Association,
members.tripod.com/gmga
Illinois Meat Goat Producers, ilmeatgoat.org
Iowa Meat Goat Association, iowameatgoat.com
Kansas Meat Goat Association, kmgaonline.net
Junior Louisiana Meat Goat Association, jlga.org
Missouri Meat Goat Producers Association,
meatgoatproducers.com
New Mexico Meat Goat Association, nmmga.org
(*New York*) Empire State Meat Goat Producers
 Association, esmgpa.org
North Carolina Meat Goat Association, ncmeatgoat.com
(*Ohio*) Buckeye Meat Goat Marketing Alliance,
ohiomarketgoat.com
Oklahoma Youth Meat Goat Assocation,
oklahomameatgoatassociation.com
Oregon Meat Goat Producers, omgp.org
Pennsylvania Meat Goat Producers Association,
pmgpa.org
South Carolina Meat Goat Association, scmga.tripod.com

## *Regional Meat Goat Associations in the U.S.*

**Heartland Meat Goat Producers Association,** (*Iowa, Minnesota, Michigan, Wisconsin*), hmgpa.tripod.com

**Meat Goat Producers Association** (*Southeast Kansas and Northeast Oklahoma*), mgpa-sek-neo.com

**Mid-South Meat Goat Association** (*Arkansas, Missouri*), midsouthmeatgoatassociation.com

**Mills County Meat Goat Association** (*Texas*), mcmga.org

**Mountain States Meat Goat Association,** (*Colorado, Idaho, Montana, Nebraska, Nevada, Utah, Wyoming*) msmga.org

**MPWV Meat Goat Producers Association** (*Maryland, Pennsylvania, West Virginia*), meatgoat.biz

**North Arkansas Meat Goat Association,** arkansasmeatgoat.com

**North Central Texas Meat Goat Association,** nctmga.com

**Snake River Meat Goat Association,** (*Idaho, Oregon, Washington, and Nevada*), srmga.com

**Tall Corn Meat Wether Association** (*Iowa*), meatgoatwether.com

## Boer Goat Associations in the U.S.

American Boer Goat Association, abga.org
Cascade Boer Goat Association (*Oregon, Washington*),
  cascadebga.org
Midwest Boer Goat Breeders Club (*Indiana, Iowa, Illinois,*
 *Michigan, Minnesota, Missouri, Ohio, Wisconsin*),
          mbgbc.com
Northwest Boer Goat Association (*Idaho, Oregon,*
 *Washington*), nwboergoatassn.org
Northeast Texas Goat Raisers Association, netgra.com
Ohio Boer Goat Association, ohioboergoatassociation.com
Oklahoma Boer Goat Association, obga.org

## National and Regional Goat Associations in Australia

Boer Goat Breeders Association of Australia,
       australianboergoat.com.au
Dairy Goat Society of Australia, dairygoats.org.au
Dairy Goat Society of Australia Tasmanian Branch,
        dgsatas.com
Goat Industry Council of Australia, gica.com.au
Goats Now, goatsnow.com.au

## National and Regional Goat Associations in Canada

Alberta Goat Breeders Association, albertagoatbreeders.ca
Canadian Goat Society, goats.ca
Canadian Meat Goat Association, canadianmeatgoat.com
Canadian National Goat Federation, cangoats.com
Ontario Goat Breeders Association, ogba.ca
Ontario Goat Milk Producers' Association,
ontariogoatmilk.org

## National Goat Association in Denmark

Dansk Økologisk Gedeavlerforening (Danish Organic Goat Breeders' Association), dansk-okoged.dk

## National Goat Association in Ireland

Irish Goat Producers Association, irishgoatproducers.com

## National Goat Associations in New Zealand

New Zealand Boer Goat Breeders Association,
boergoatassn.co.nz
New Zealand Dairy Goat Breeders, nzdgba.co.nz

## National Goat Associations in South Africa

Boer Goats – South Africa, boergoats.co.za
South Africa Milch Goat Breeders' Society,
sa-breeders.co.za/org/milch-goats

## National Goat Associations in the U.K.

British Boer Goat Society, britishboergoatsociety.co.uk
British Goat Society (*founded 1879*), allgoats.com

## International Goat Association

International Goat Association, iga-goatworld.org

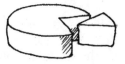

# The Cheese Stands Alone

Goat cheese, sometimes called *chèvre*, is a product made from the milk of goats. Goat cheese has been made for thousands of years, and was probably one of the earliest made dairy products.

Goat cheese comes in a wide variety of forms, although the most common is a soft, easily spread cheese. Goat cheese can also be made in hard aged varieties as well as semi-firm cheeses like feta. Goat cheese is especially common in the Middle East, Africa, and Mediterranean countries, where the hardy goat survives in areas where cows cannot.

Although the West has popularized the cow, goat milk and goat cheese are preferred dairy products in much of the rest of the world.

Because goat milk is leaner than that of cows, goat cheese tends to be leaner as well. For this reason, many dieters craving cheese will use goat cheese as a substitute, crumbling it on salads, or melting it on cooked dishes. Goat cheese softens when exposed to heat, although it does not melt in the same way that many cow cheeses do. Firmer goat cheeses with rinds are sometimes baked in the oven to form a gooey warm cheese which is ideal for spreading on bread or alone.

We are proud of our Central Oregon cheese producers who have garnered quite a few awards for their efforts. Two of them, Tumalo Farms and Junioer Grove Farm, deserve a special mention.

# Getting Your Goat

**Tumalo Farms**, tumalofarms.com
Tumalo Farms *Classico* is an award-winning cheese. This *Classico* is an unpasteurized version of the cheese that has become their standard. It is made with fresh goat milk in small batches to keep the affinage (maturity) more refined.

**Juniper Grove Farm**, junipergrovefarm.com
Juniper Grove Farms features a line of silky goats' cheeses, like Cumin Tomme, Gruyère by Goat, and Raw Milk Goat Feta.

**Harley Farms Goat Dairy**, harleyfarms.com
Harley Farms isn't in Oregon, but we can't hold that against them…. Do be sure to look at this website and, if you are in the area. do visit Harley Farms in Pescadero, California (see page 120 above).

And if you happen to be on the other side of the pond, there are some stunning cheeses to be had.…

## Goat Cheese in Ireland

**CÁIS: Irish Farmhouse Cheesemakers Association,**
irishcheese.ie
**Directory of Irish Farmhouse Cheeses**
forkandbottle.com/cheese

## Goat Cheese in the U.K.

**The Cheese Society**, thecheesesociety.co.uk

# Index

# Getting Your Goat

# Index

# Getting Your Goat

# How to Order this Book

# How to Order this Book

Additional copies of this book can be obtained in a number of ways. Online purchases can be made at **amazon.com**, **amazon.ca**, **amazon.co.uk**, **barnesandnoble.com**, and other sources. Your local bookstore will be able to order the book through its regular book distributor, such as Ingrams in North America and Gardners in Europe.

If you are a producer or vendor of goat meat or cheese and wish to have copies of the book to sell at farmer's markets, specialty stores, meat markets, and so on, you can purchase multiple copies at a discount.

| | |
|---|---|
| 5–9 copies | 5% discount |
| 10–19 copies | 10% discount |
| 20–29 copies | 20% discount |
| 30–39 copies | 30% discount |
| 40–49 copies | 35% discount |
| 50 or more copies | 40% discount |

Simply send an e-mail to **goat@evertype.com** with the number of copies you want to purchase along with your name and shipping address and we will send you a quotation on the price, including shipping. We accept advance payment by PayPal. If you need a rush order, that can be accommodated at additional cost.

# Notes